P9-DTO-273

TOUT de SUITE

à la

MICROWAVE

by

JEAN K DURKEE

A gourmet's cookbook of French, Acadian & Creole recipes

1st printing	December, 1977	7,500 copies
2nd printing	February, 1978	15,000 copies
3rd printing	July, 1978	30,000 copies
4th printing	March, 1979	40,000 copies
5th printing	May, 1980	40,000 copies
6th printing	December, 1980	60,000 copies
7th printing	September, 1982	80,000 copies

ISBN   0-9605362-0-5
Library of Congress Catalog Card Number 77-93096

Copyright © 1977 by Jean K. Durkee
Tout de Suite à la Microwave
P. O. Box 30121
Lafayette
Louisiana
70503

All Rights Reserved

This book, including any part thereof,
may not be reproduced
by any means or utilized in any other manner or form
without the written consent of the author.

*To my husband, Bob, who gave Tout de Suite
its name and encouraged me to compile a
collection of recipes from Louisiana,
and our sons Robert, Mark and Todd.*

ACKNOWLEDGEMENTS

Recipes developed and tested by:
Jean Durkee, Ruby Gueno, Doreen Duhé,
Billie Hebert and Mary Kathryn Scott

Illustrations:
Randy Herpin

Photography:
Maurice Perea

Editorial Consultant:
Patricia L. Dakin

Typist:
Rose Must

French translation:
Dave Domingue and Annick St. Hubert Colbert

Historical research:
Louise Hanchey, Beverly Latimer and Ruth Bowen
Material on file at the
Lafayette Natural History Museum

Index:
Jolene Levermann

Published by
Tout de Suite a la Microwave, Inc.
P.O. Box 30121
Lafayette, Louisiana 70503

Printed in U.S.A.
S.C. Toof & Co.
Memphis, Tennessee

Introduction

Bonjour microwave cooks,

Recipes never become obsolete, just the methods of cooking them!

Roux is a good example of cooking an "old" recipe by a "new" method. The recipe for **Roux,** the base for gumbos and stews, was brought to Louisiana by French and Acadian settlers over 200 years ago. The method of cooking a roux was to stir an equal mixture of flour and oil constantly in a black iron pot until a dark brown color was achieved.

Now, with the Microwave, many changes have been made. First of all, a beautiful dark brown roux can be microwaved in a 4-cup glass measuring cup in 7 minutes. With the addition of chopped vegetables microwaved 5 minutes more, the perfect roux will be ready in 12 minutes. If you have ever stirred and watched a roux, so as not to burn it, you will appreciate the quickness of your new cooking method. Also, you will enjoy the ease of washing a glass measuring cup versus the "black iron pot."

Peanut Brittle is another excellent example of fast cooking—one pound in only 9 minutes! Economical, too—less than fifty cents a pound. Not to be outdone, **Fudge, Tout de Suite** cooks itself in 2 minutes. These are really fun to make.

All of the 197 nutritional, economical and colorful recipes in **Tout de Suite à la Microwave** were developed and tested in 600-675 watt Microwaves in home kitchens. I tested two-thirds of the recipes and the other one-third were tested by qualified enthusiastic friends listed in acknowledgments. Three power settings were used in testing the recipes: **LOW/DEFROST, MEDIUM/SLO COOK** and **HIGH** power. Various sized glass, ceramic and microsafe plastic utensils were used in testing and are indicated along with cooking time and number of servings for each recipe to aid you in obtaining the best results with your microwave cooking. Before you begin microwaving, read the user's manual which came with your oven. It contains specific information which you will find helpful.

A positive attitude is necessary in microwave cooking. Although your Microwave can do extraordinary feats, you control the machine and the food that is prepared. So, use your imagination, have fun with these recipes and be ready to accept compliments on your "fabulous cooking."

Cookbooks should not be just for cooking, but should lift the spirit and convey new ideas. I hope, through my enthusiasm for microwave cooking, you will be inspired to experiment with your own family recipes, using **Tout de Suite** as a guide.

Jean Kellner Durkee

Table of Contents

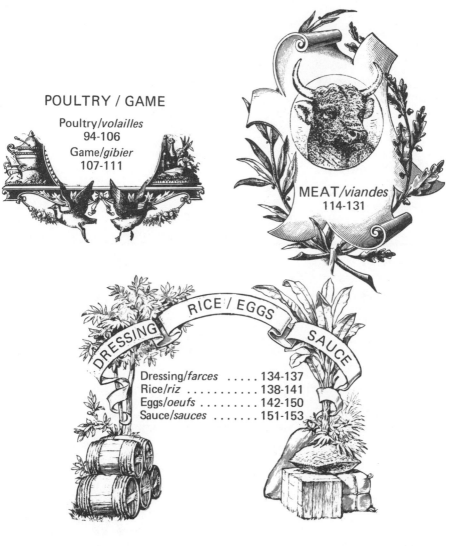

Utensils

Ninety percent of the microwave safe utensils needed for *Tout de Suite* recipes are probably in your kitchen cabinets now. The following utensils are suggestions to help you in microwave cooking.

UTENSIL OR CONTAINER	SIZE	A FEW OF THE RECIPES CALLING FOR THIS UTENSIL
Glass measuring cups (preferably with a handle) for cooking and serving in other containers	2-cup 4-cup 8-cup	Roux, peanut brittle, fudge, sauces, sautéing mushrooms, onions, celery and other chopped vegetables, prepared soup, grits.
Round glass casseroles for cooking and serving	1 quart 1½ quart 2 quart 2½ quart	Vegetables, dips, fruit, cakes, puddings, custards, casseroles, sauces, steamed seafood, rice. By placing a small juice glass in the center of the cake mixture in a 2 quart dish, a good bundt dish is created.
Corning casseroles for cooking and serving	3 quart 4 quart or 5 quart	Meat, poultry, game, seafood, maquechou, jambalaya, dressing, étouffée, stews, gumbo, soup, casseroles, artichokes, spaghetti meat sauce, vegetables.
Corning skillet for cooking and serving	10″	Very versatile for fish, lasagna, dressings, bananas Foster, stuffed peppers, chicken, ducks, dove.
Browning skillet/ combination covered casserole dish for cooking and serving	2 quart 9″ x 9″	Searing and browning steaks, hamburgers and all cuts of meat, game and poultry. Fried eggs, French toast, corn bread. For quick clean up, baking soda removes all brown areas in skillet.
Corning or glass loaf dish for cooking and serving	5″ x 9″	Country terrine, oysters in a blanket, reheating frozen rice, steamed lobster tails, fruit, fish, spice cake.
Glass pie plates Ceramic Quiche dish for Cooking and Serving	9-10″ 10″	Pies, omelets, quiche, corn bread, brownies, meat loaf, roasted peanuts and pecans, ham loaf.

Utensils

Remember, utensils or dishes with metal or metallic trim are harmful to your Microwave.

UTENSIL OR CONTAINER	SIZE	A FEW OF THE RECIPES CALLING FOR THIS UTENSIL
Round glass cake dish with 2" high sides for Cooking and Serving	8" 9"	Layered cakes and small casseroles, steamed artichokes, stuffed peppers, stuffed tomatoes, fruit, bread pudding.
Glass ramekins	6 oz. 8 oz.	Eggs, custard, individual casseroles for seafood.
Scallop shells and oyster shells		Hors d'oeuvre, seafood, oysters Bienville and Rockefeller.
Dinner plates	without metal trim	Bacon, chicken livers wrapped in bacon, bacon sticks (use paper towel to absorb fat), reheating entire meal.
Glass utility dish	7"x11" 8" x 8"	Coca cola cake, casseroles, fruit, reheating and bananas Foster.
Microwave safe plastic dishes		Bundt cake, bacon, layer cakes, rack for roast.

COVERS		FOODS TO COVER
Wax paper	to fit top of dish loosely	1) Those with high fat content to prevent spattering.
Lid for dish	size according to dish	2) Eggs 3) Those to be simmered.
Plastic wrap	enclose, do not let food touch or plastic will soften and melt	4) Those to be steamed. Be careful when removing plastic covering because the container is filled with hot steam.
Paper towels or napkins	layers	5) Bread—moisture is readily absorbed with paper towels. Bacon—to absorb fat.
Vegetable paper or plastic packaging	puncture carton	6) Frozen—to distribute heat evenly.

MICRO MEMOS

SIZE AND SHAPE OF COOKING CONTAINER: Use round or oval containers. Food cooked in square or rectangular dishes absorb more energy in the corners and do not cook evenly. Roux and sauces cook faster in small containers (such as measuring cups) than in large containers where the mixture is spread out.

ARRANGEMENT OF FOOD: Food will cook more evenly if arranged in a circle either in a container or in the microwave without a container (such as potatoes). The meatier portions of poultry or meat should be placed toward the outside of the dish with the bony parts in the center.

STARTING TEMPERATURE: Cooking times for *Tout de Suite* recipes were determined with food at room temperature unless stated "frozen." Frozen vegetables cook evenly in the paper carton without stirring or turning. Remove printed waxed outer paper and place carton on a plate for easy removal from the microwave. Season after cooking.

DENSITY OF FOOD: Foods which are porous and have low density and low moisture content, such as bread and pastry, absorb microwave energy and cook quickly. Foods containing high levels of sugar or fat also cook quickly. Dense and moist food such as roast beef and ham require more energy and longer microwave cooking time.

LIQUID: Microwave energy goes to the liquid in a dish, therefore, the liquid juices from roasts and water-laden vegetables, such as squash, zucchini and eggplant, should be drained off during cooking.

SALT: Salt draws out moisture. If you don't want a lot of liquid, add salt after cooking, especially on meat, poultry and seafood.

STIRRING: Stirring is important, especially for sauces, soups and vegetables. The food on the outer edge of the dish, which is cooking faster, needs to be mixed with the food in the center. Wooden spoons can be left in the mixture which needs to be stirred often.

ROTATING: Rotating or turning the dish is important for even cooking, especially for meats, cakes and fruits.

THERMOMETERS: Thermometers which are made especially for microwave use are not designed for regular oven usage.

MICRO MEMOS

FREEZING AND DEFROSTING: Plan and store leftovers so that they may be conveniently frozen and reheated in the microwave. Freeze gumbo and soup in glass jars which will fit in the microwave for future defrosting. *Freezing Hint: Place lid on the jar after food has expanded and frozen.* Remove lid before defrosting. Wax paper can be used as a cover to stop spatters. Follow defrost/timing directions in your microwave manual. If food or liquid has been frozen in plastic containers which are not microwave safe, transfer the food to a glass or Corning dish for defrosting. Plastic will warp or melt if the food being defrosted has a high fat content.

CONVERTING RECIPES: Once you master a few cooking techniques and become accustomed to the quickness of microwave cooking, it will be easier to convert your favorite recipes. Two important things to do in converting recipes are (1) reduce the liquid by 1/4 (if the recipe calls for 1 cup of liquid, reduce this to 3/4 cup) and (2) change cooking time to 1/4 of the conventional cooking time.

TIMING: The energy to supply cooking appliances and your own energy are two very special resources. Since saving energy is one of the most important advantages of microwave cooking, you should want to use your microwave to full capacity. Think of *Tout de Suite* as a cooking lesson or guide and select a menu each day from the recipes. Plan and organize your defrosting and cooking time so everything is ready to serve at the same time. An example of planning:
1) Cook soup or gumbo earlier in the day (seasoning will blend throughout).
2) If the dessert needs to be chilled, it can be prepared early, also.
3) Later, prepare the main dish. Casseroles can be completed up to the final step and reheated before serving; roast, chicken or ham will store heat if kept covered after cooking.
4) Cook potatoes next. After cooking, wrap in foil to keep warm.
5) Finally, cook the vegetables.
6) Heat the casserole and soup.
Dinner is now ready to be served in the attractive containers used for cooking. The kitchen is still cool and cleanup is a breeze.

Hors d'oeuvre

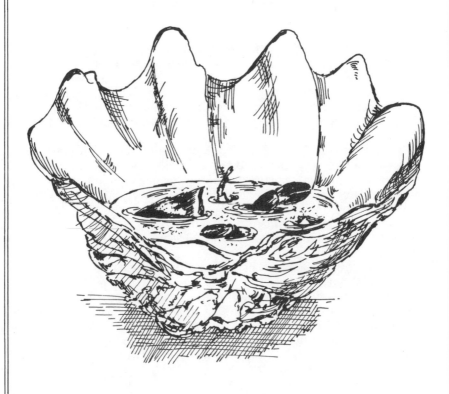

Hors d'oeuvre:
Hors d'oeuvre and appetizers can set the stage for a memorable meal. These are fun to make and a delight to eat!

ARTICHOKE DIP/crème d'artichauts

Cooking Time: 5 to 8 minutes
Utensil: 2 quart dish

2 (14 oz.) cans artichoke
    hearts, drained and
    finely chopped
8 oz. Parmesan cheese,
    grated
1 pint mayonnaise

Mix chopped artichokes with cheese and mayonnaise in a 2 quart glass dish. Microwave on **HIGH 5 TO 8 MINUTES,** stirring once, until bubbly. Serve with crackers.

STUFFED ARTICHOKES/artichauts farcis

Cooking Time: 25 minutes
Utensils: glass or ceramic plate
8-cup measuring cup
Servings: 4

4 artichokes

1. Wash, cut bottoms from artichokes and trim leaf tips. Place artichokes in a plastic bag, twisting end to close bag. For easy removal, place bag on a plate. Microwave on **HIGH 14 to 16 MINUTES.** Turn dish 2 times. Salt may be sprinkled on after cooking. Let stand covered 3 mintues.

STUFFING

1/2 cup butter or margarine
2 cups green onions,
**   chopped**
4 cloves garlic, minced
1 cup parsley, chopped
**   fine**
1 cup seasoned bread crumbs
1 cup grated parmesan
**   cheese**

2. Melt butter or margarine in an 8-cup glass measure on **HIGH 1 MINUTE.** Sauté onions and garlic in butter on **HIGH 4 MINUTES.** Add parsley, bread crumbs and cheese. Mix well.

Fill each leaf of artichoke with bread crumb mixture starting with bottom leaves. When ready to serve, microwave stuffed artichokes **4 MINUTES ON HIGH.**

Stuffed artichokes can be wrapped individually in plastic wrap and frozen.

BACON STICKS/baguettes au bacon

Cooking Time: 2 minutes
Utensils: paper plate
　　　　　　paper towels
Servings: 4

2 slices bacon, cut
　　lengthwise to make
　　4 strips
4 bread sticks

1. Wrap bacon around bread sticks (barber's pole fashion). Place on paper plate and paper towel to absorb fat. Cover with paper towel. Cook on **HIGH 2 MINUTES.**

2. Place sticks in a mug to serve.

NACHOS

Cooking Time: 1-2 minutes
Utensil: plate
Servings: 3

Tortilla chips
Sharp cheddar cheese,
　　grated
Jalapeno peppers,
　　sliced

1. Place a layer of chips, about 15, on a plate. Sprinkle with grated cheese. Slice peppers thin, and place over cheese.

2. Cook on **LOW FOR 2 MINUTES** or until cheese melts. Nachos can be cooked on **HIGH FOR 1 MIN-UTE.** Serve hot.

MARINATED BRUSSELS SPROUTS
choux de Bruxelles marinées

Cooking Time: 7 minutes
Utensil: paper carton
Servings: 4-6

1 (10 oz.) package frozen
  Baby Brussels Sprouts

1. Pierce box and cook Brussels sprouts in package on **HIGH 7 MINUTES** or until tender. Drain and cool.

1/2 cup Italian dressing
1/2 teaspoon dillweed
1/2 cup green bell pepper,
  chopped

2. Mix together Italian dressing, dillweed and green peppers. Pour over Brussels sprouts and marinate for at least 24 hours. Serve with wooden picks.

CAPANADA

Cooking Time: 1 hour 15 minutes
Utensil: 4 quart casserole
Makes 2 quarts

3 cups onion, coarsely
    chopped
1-1/2 cups bell pepper,
    coarsely chopped
1-1/2 cups celery, coarsely
    chopped
1/2 cup olive oil

1. In a 4 quart casserole, sauté onion, bell pepper and celery in olive oil. Cover with wax paper and cook on **HIGH 30 MINUTES.** Stir once or twice.

2 large eggplants, peeled
    and cut in 1" cubes.
    Soak in salt water 20
    minutes, drain.
1 (8 oz.) can tomato sauce
1 (6 oz.) can tomato paste

2. Stir in eggplant. Cover and cook on **HIGH 30 MINUTES.** Stir once. Add tomato sauce and paste. Cook on **HIGH 10 MINUTES.**

5 cloves garlic, minced
1 (6 oz.) can pitted black
    olives, whole
1/2 cup pitted green olives,
    whole
1/2 cup red wine vinegar
3 Tablespoons sugar
1/4 cup capers
1-1/2 teaspoons oregano
1 Tablespoon salt
1 teaspoon cayenne pepper
1 teaspoon pepper

3. Stir in garlic, olives, vinegar, sugar, capers, oregano, salt and peppers. Cook on **HIGH 5 MINUTES.** Chill before serving.

Serve Capanada with crackers or slices of French bread.

16

HOT CLAM DIP/sauce de palourde

Cooking Time: 7 minutes
Utensil: 1 quart covered glass dish
Makes 3 cups

2 (6½ oz.) cans minced clams, drain and reserve ¼ cup liquid

1. Place clams and ¼ cup clam liquid in a 1 quart covered glass dish. Microwave on **HIGH 5 MINUTES.**

**12 oz. cream cheese, softened
1/2 cup butter, softened**

2. Stir cream cheese and butter into clams. Cook on **HIGH 1½-2 MINUTES.** Stir until smooth. Serve hot with crackers or chips.

CHEESE PETIT-FOURS

Cooking Time: 3 minutes per batch
Utensil: round glass plate
Makes 5 dozen

3 (1 pound) loaves Pepperidge Farm sandwich bread (square loaf)

1. Cut crust off 2½ loaves bread (3 slices at a time).

**1 pound margarine (4 sticks)
4 (5 oz.) jars Kraft Old English cheese spread
1½ teaspoons Worcestershire sauce
1 teaspoon Tabasco
1 teaspoon onion powder
dash of cayenne pepper**

dill weed and cayenne pepper for topping

2. Beat margarine, cheese spread, Worcestershire, Tabasco, onion powder and cayenne pepper with a rotary beater or process with the steel blade in a food processor until consistency of icing. Spread cheese mixture between each layer of bread. Quarter. Each petit-four is three slices thick. Spread cheese all over sides and top of each quarter. Sprinkle dill weed and cayenne over top of each petit-four. Freeze petit-fours on cookie sheet. Transfer to plastic bags for convenience and return to freezer. When ready to serve, place 12 frozen petit-fours on a glass plate. Cover with wax paper (optional). Cook on **HIGH 3 MINUTES.** Turn dish once. Serve hot from the microwave.

17

CHICKEN LIVERS/WATER CHESTNUTS WRAPPED IN BACON
Marinated in Teriyaki Sauce

Cooking Time: 18 minutes
Utensils: plate, paper towels
Servings: 36

Teriyaki sauce
1/2 pound chicken livers,
   cut in 36 pieces

12 slices lean bacon,
   cut in thirds
1 (6 oz.) can water
   chestnuts, cut in
   36 pieces

1. Marinate livers in Teriyaki sauce overnight.

2. Cut livers, bacon and water chestnuts in 36 pieces each. Wrap a piece of bacon around liver and water chestnut. Secure with a wooden pick—try to pierce the water chestnut.

3. Place 12 at a time on a plate lined with paper towels. Cover with a paper towel. Cook on **HIGH 6 MINUTES** or until bacon is crisp. Turn plate once during cooking time.

CRABMEAT DIP/crème de crabe
Hot or Cold

Cooking Time: 8 minutes
Utensil: 2 quart dish
Servings: 8-10

1/2 cup butter, melted
1/4 cup onion, chopped
2 Tablespoons parsley,
    chopped
1/4 cup celery, chopped
8 oz. cream cheese

1. In a 2 quart dish, sauté butter, onion, parsley and celery on **HIGH 4 MINUTES.** Stir in cream cheese. Microwave on **HIGH 1 MINUTE** if cheese is not softened.

1/8 teaspoon garlic
    powder
1/4 teaspoon Tabasco
1/2 teaspoon salt
1 Tablespoon Worcester-
    shire sauce

2. Add garlic powder, Tabasco, salt and Worcestershire sauce, mix well.

1 pound white crabmeat

3. Fold crabmeat in gently. Microwave on **HIGH 4 MINUTES.** Serve with miniature patty shells or melba rounds.

CRAWFISH AU GRATIN/écrevisses au gratin

Serve as a dip with melba rounds or as an entrée in pastry shells.

Cooking Time: 11 minutes
Utensil: 2 quart casserole
Servings: 6

2 Tablespoons butter
1 bunch green onion tops,
   chopped

1. Sauté onions and butter in a 2 quart casserole on **HIGH 3 MINUTES.**

2 Tablespoons flour
1/2 cup whipping cream
1/4 cup white wine
1 teaspoon salt
1 teaspoon cayenne pepper
1/4 teaspoon Tabasco
1/4 teaspoon garlic powder

2. Add flour, cream and wine, salt, pepper, Tabasco and garlic. Cook on **HIGH 1½-2 MINUTES.**

6 oz. American cheese,
   grated
3 oz. Swiss cheese,
   grated
1 pound peeled crawfish
   tails

3. Stir cheese into hot mixture until it is melted. Add crawfish. Cover with wax paper and cook on **HIGH 6 MINUTES.** Stir halfway through cooking time.

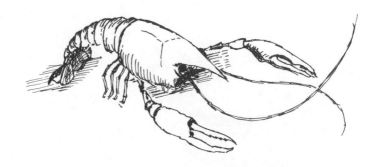

ESCARGOTS A LA BOURGUIGNONNE

Cooking Time: 4 minutes
Utensils: 2 dozen snail shells, 4 ceramic dishes
Servings: 4 (6 each)

1/2 cup butter
2 cloves garlic, mashed
2 Tablespoons parsley, minced
1 teaspoon Tony's (or your favorite) Creole seasoning
1/4 teaspoon lemon juice
2 dozen canned snails

1. Cream butter and add garlic, parsley, seasoning and lemon juice. Put ¼ teaspoon of garlic butter into shell, then push in snail (tail end first). Push as far as it will go. Cover with another ¼ teaspoon of garlic butter. Refrigerate filled shells several hours or overnight.

2. Place 6 shells in 4 ceramic Escargot dishes or saucers and cover loosely with plastic wrap. Place 6 shells at a time in microwave and cook on **HIGH 1 MINUTE** or until butter bubbles.

Serve with warm French bread. Place the escargot on bread to eat and dip remainder of bread in sauce.

MUSHROOMS EVANGELINE
champignons evangeline

Cooking Time: 10 minutes
Utensil: 2 quart casserole
Servings: 4

1 pound fresh mushrooms

1/4 cup butter, melted
1 Tablespoon marjoram
1 Tablespoon chives,
minced
1 cup chicken bouillon
1/4 cup dry white wine
1/4 teaspoon salt
freshly ground pepper

1. Wash and dry mushrooms and place in a 2 quart casserole.

2. Melt butter in a 4-cup measure. Add marjoram, chives, bouillon, wine, salt and pepper. Pour over mushrooms. Microwave on **HIGH 10 MINUTES** or until mushrooms are tender.

MUSHROOMS IN GARLIC BUTTER
champignons au beurre d'ail

Cooking Time: 2 to 4 minutes
Utensil: round glass baking dish
Servings: 6-8

1/2 cup butter
1 Tablespoon green onion
tops, finely chopped
3 cloves garlic, pressed
or minced
2 Tablespoons parsley,
finely chopped
dash of seasoned pepper

1. Blend butter, onion, garlic, parsley and pepper. Cover and chill. Unused garlic butter can be kept in refrigerator.

1 pound fresh mushrooms

2. Rinse mushrooms, dry and remove stems (reserve for other recipes). Fill each cap with ¼ teaspoon garlic butter and arrange in a round glass serving dish. Cook 1 or 2 dozen mushrooms, uncovered, on **HIGH 2 TO 4 MINUTES.** Rotate dish once.

MUSHROOMS SUPREME/champignons suprêmes

Cooking Time: 14 minutes
Utensil: 2 quart glass dish
Servings: 6

1/2 cup butter

1. Micromelt butter in a 2 quart glass dish on **HIGH 1 MINUTE.**

2 cups onion, diced
1 beef or chicken
   bouillon cube
1 teaspoon garlic powder
1 teaspoon seasoned pepper

2. Sauté onion, bouillon cube, garlic powder and pepper in butter. Cover and cook on **HIGH 8 MIN-UTES.** Stir after ½ of cooking time.

1 pound fresh mushrooms
   (rinsed and dried)
1/4 cup red wine

3. Add mushrooms and wine. Cover. Cook on **HIGH 5 MINUTES.**

ROASTED PEANUTS/cacahuêtes

Cooking Time: 5 minutes 10 seconds
Utensil: glass pie plate

2 cups unshelled raw peanuts

Place peanuts in a glass pie plate. Microwave on **HIGH 2 MINUTES 35 SECONDS.** Stir. Cook **2 MINUTES 35 SECONDS** longer.

ROASTED PECANS/pacanes rôties

Cooking Time: 4 to 5 minutes
Utensil: glass pie plate

1 cup pecan halves

Place pecans in a glass pie plate. Microwave on **HIGH 2 MINUTES.** Stir. Cook on **HIGH 2 MORE MINUTES.** Stir, let rest 2 minutes then taste. If you like a more roasted flavor, 1 more minute should do it. Sprinkle on salt if desired.

SEAFOOD DIP/crème fruit de mer

Cooking Time: 14 minutes
Utensil: 3 quart dish
Makes 2 quarts

1 cup onion, chopped
1 clove garlic, chopped
1/4 cup green bell pepper,
   chopped
1/4 cup butter, melted

1. In a 3 quart dish, sauté onion, garlic and pepper in butter, covered, on **HIGH 8 MINUTES** or until vegetables are limp.

2 Tablespoons flour
20 oz. bottle catsup
1/2 pound velveeta cheese,
   diced
1 teaspoon salt
1/4 teaspoon pepper
1/4 teaspoon cayenne
   pepper
1/4 teaspoon hot pepper
   sauce

2. Stir in flour, catsup, cheese, salt, pepper, and hot pepper sauce. Microwave on **HIGH 1 MINUTE** to melt cheese.

2 (10 oz.) jars oysters,
   drain and reserve
   liquid
1 pound claw crabmeat
1 pound small, cooked
   shrimp, peeled

3. Fold in oysters, crab and shrimp. Microwave on **HIGH 5 MINUTES** covered until heated through. Add small amount of oyster liquid if mixture is too thick.

   Serve with white melba rounds.

STEAMED OYSTERS/huîtres étuvées

Cooking Time: 4 minutes
Servings: 6

6 fresh oysters, in unopened shell (rinse off shells)

Place 6 oysters in the microwave. Heat on **HIGH 4 MINUTES** or until shells open.

Dip cooked oysters in melted butter or your favorite sauce.

STEAMED SHRIMP/crevettes étuvées

Shrimp can be peeled before or after cooking.

Cooking Time: 7 minutes
Utensil: 2 quart glass dish
Servings: 4

**1 pound shrimp,
   fresh or frozen
1/2 teaspoon cayenne
   pepper
1/2 lemon sliced
1/2 onion, sliced
1 rib celery, cut up
NO WATER!
1 teaspoon salt**

Place shrimp and all the seasonings except salt in a glass dish. Cover with wax paper. Cook on **HIGH 7 MINUTES** until all shrimp are pink. Stir after half of cooking time. Add salt. Let stand 3 minutes. Test for doneness—shrimp should be tender and pink.

SWEET AND SOUR SAUSAGE
saucisses amer-sucrées

Cooking Time: 7 minutes
Utensil: 2 quart glass dish
Servings: 8-10

1 pound smoked sausage,
cut in ½" slices
1/2 cup hot water

1. Cut sausage and place in a 2 quart dish. Add hot water, cover and cook on **HIGH 5 MINUTES**. Drain.

2/3 cup chutney,
(Chut-Nut if available)
1 cup sour cream

2. Stir in chutney and sour cream. Reheat before serving on **MEDIUM 2 MINUTES**. Sausage can be served in glass cooking dish or chafing dish with wooden picks.

VENISON SAUSAGE BALLS/venaison et saucisses

Cooking Time: 45 seconds per sausage
Utensils: Bacon rack or round plate
paper towels

1 pound ground venison
sausage

Roll sausage in small balls and place on the outer edge of bacon rack or round plate with paper towels under and over sausage. Microwave 45 seconds for each sausage ball. Use chart for approximate timing. If sausage has a lot of fat, pour off and continue cooking.

Sausage Balls	Cooking Time
3	2 mins. 15 sec.
6	4 mins. 30 sec.
9	6 mins. 45 sec.
12	9 mins.

29

Roux
Gumbo
Soup

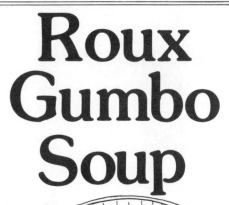

Roux:
   Of course, as every Louisiana cook knows—to make a good roux is to be a good cook. So, relax, the microwave can do it for you in just seven minutes!

Gumbo:
   No one really knows where the delicious gumbos of the bayou land began. Recipes for gumbo requiring five to seven hours cooking time can be found in the first Louisiana cookbooks printed in New Orleans in 1885. Now, with a little help from the Microwave and liberal dashes of hot pepper sauce, the good taste of a recipe from the past can be enjoyed in much less time!

Soup:
   One of the first pleasures of a successful meal is a savory soup. You might be tempted to make soup the entire meal!

ROUX

ROUX is an equal mixture of oil and flour that is browned and used as a thickening base for many of the South Louisiana dishes such as stews, gumbos, étouffées and sauce piquantes. It not only thickens, but it also gives a different, quite distinct flavor due to the browning of the flour.

Cooking Time: 12 minutes
Utensil: 4-cup glass measuring cup
Makes 4 cups

2/3 cup oil
2/3 cup flour

1. Mix oil and flour together in a 4-cup measure. Microwave uncovered on **HIGH 6-7 MINUTES.** Stir at 6 minutes — Roux will be a light brown at this time and will need to cook 30 seconds to 1 minute longer to reach the dark brown color so important in making Louisiana gumbos and stews. The Roux will be very hot, but usually the handle on your glass measuring cup will stay cool enough to touch.

2 cups onion, chopped
1 cup celery, chopped
1/2 cup green bell pepper, chopped

2. Add onion, celery and bell pepper to Roux in measuring cup. Stir and return to Microwave. Sauté on **HIGH 3 MINUTES.**

4 cloves garlic, minced
1/4 cup parsley, chopped
1/4 cup green onion tops, chopped

3. Add garlic, parsley and green onion to Roux, stir and return to Microwave. Sauté on **HIGH 2 MINUTES.**

You should have about 3-3/4 cups of Roux now. If any oil has risen to the top, pour this off.

Approximately 1/4 cup hot water

4. Slowly add enough hot tap water to bring Roux to the 4-cup mark. Stir and you will have a smooth dark Roux in only 12 minutes.

Roux freezes very well and you are ready at any time to put together a delicious gumbo or stew.

CHICKEN AND SAUSAGE GUMBO
de poulet et de saucisse

Cooking Time: Roux — 12 minutes
                      Gumbo — 20 minutes
Utensils: 4-cup glass measuring cup
                5 quart casserole
Servings: 8-10

2½ pound chicken
   cooked

1. Cook chicken (page 104). Strain and reserve stock.

2/3 cup oil } Roux
2/3 cup flour }

2. Prepare Roux with 2/3 cup oil and 2/3 cup flour. Cook on **HIGH 7 MINUTES** in a 4-cup measure and follow complete directions for adding vegetables to the Roux on page 32.

4 cups hot water
3 cups chicken stock
2 teaspoons salt
1/2 teaspoon pepper
1/4 teaspoon cayenne
   pepper

3. Place Roux in a 5 quart casserole. Stir in hot water, stock and seasonings. Cover. Cook on **HIGH 10 MINUTES.**

2 cups cooked chicken,
   (cut in bite size)
1 pound sausage, cut
   in 1" slices

4. Add chicken and sausage. Cook on **HIGH 10 MINUTES.** Serve over rice.

CHICKEN OKRA GUMBO/de poulet et d'okra

This gumbo is quick if you cook the chicken and okra ahead of time. See the index for these two Tout de Suite recipes.

Cooking Time: Roux — 12 minutes
                    Gumbo — 30 minutes
Utensils: 5 quart casserole
              4-cup glass measuring cup
Servings: 8-10

2/3 cup oil ⎫ **Roux**
2/3 cup flour ⎭

4 cups hot water
3 cups chicken stock
2 cups cooked chicken
2 cups okra, cooked or
    canned

1 Tablespoon salt
1 teaspoon pepper
1/2 teaspoon cayenne
    pepper

1. Prepare Roux with 2/3 cup oil and 2/3 cup flour. Cook on **HIGH 7 MINUTES** in a 4-cup measure and follow complete directions for adding vegetables to Roux on page 32.

2. Place Roux in a 5 quart casserole. Add hot water, stock, chicken, okra.

3. Stir in seasonings.

4. Cook on **HIGH 30 MINUTES.** Serve over rice.

DURK'S DUCK AND SAUSAGE GUMBO
de canard et de saucisse

Cooking Time: Roux—12 minutes
Gumbo—50 minutes
Utensils: 3 and 5 quart casseroles
4-cup glass measuring cup
Servings: 8

3 or 4 wild ducks, cleaned
1 large onion, quartered
1/2 bunch parsley leaves
1 rib celery and leaves
1/2 teaspoon cayenne pepper
1/2 teaspoon salt
2 cups hot water

1. Cut duck into 4 pieces with poultry shears. Place in a 3 quart dish along with onion, parsley, celery, seasonings and water. Cover. Cook on **HIGH 20 MINUTES** or until duck is tender. Remove bone from duck (if desired), strain stock and reserve for gumbo. This could be done the day before and refrigerated.

2/3 cup oil } **Roux**
2/3 cup flour)

6 cups hot water
1 pound lean smoked
sausage or Andouille*
(cut in ¼" slices)
2 teaspoons salt
1/4 teaspoon cayenne pepper
1/4 teaspoon Tabasco

2. Mix oil and flour together in a 4-cup measure. Cook on **HIGH 7 MINUTES.** Follow directions on page 32 for adding vegetables to roux. Place roux in a 5 quart casserole. Stir in hot water. Add duck, duck stock (if desired), sausage, salt, pepper and Tabasco. Cover with wax paper. Cook on **HIGH 30 MINUTES.**

3. Serve in bowls over a mound of fluffy white rice along with a green salad and French bread.

ANDOUILLE* (pronounced Ahn-dewey) is a sausage made of all pork which is highly seasoned with peppers, herbs and spices. This sausage is usually salted or smoked. It can be eaten, sliced cold, or added to gumbo, jambalaya or other dishes. The origin of this sausage is France.

SEAFOOD GUMBO/de fruits de mer

Put away the heavy black iron pot.

Cooking Time: Roux — 12 minutes
Gumbo — 45 minutes
Utensils: 4-cup glass measuring cup
5 quart dish
Servings: 10-12

2/3 cup flour ⎫ Roux
2/3 cup oil ⎭

1. Mix flour and oil together in a 4-cup measure. Microwave on **HIGH 6½ TO 7 MINUTES.** Stir. Roux will be dark caramel.

2 cups onion, chopped
1 cup celery, chopped
1/2 cup green bell pepper, chopped

2. Add onion, celery and pepper. Sauté on **HIGH 3 MINUTES.** Stir.

1/2 cup green onion tops, chopped
1/4 cup parsley, chopped
4 cloves garlic, minced

3. Add onion, parsley and garlic. Sauté on **HIGH 2 MINUTES.** Add hot water to bring mixture to 4-cup mark. Pour into a 5 quart dish.

1-1/2 quarts hot water
1 Tablespoon salt
1 teaspoon cayenne pepper

4. Add hot water, salt and pepper. Cover and cook on **HIGH 15 MINUTES.**

2 pounds shrimp, raw and peeled
1 pound crabmeat or 8 small boiled and cleaned crabs
1 pint oysters with liquid

5. Add shrimp and crab. Cover and cook on **MEDIUM 20 MINUTES.** Add oysters and liquid — cook on **MEDIUM 10 MINUTES.** Serve with rice and Filé.

SHRIMP GUMBO/de crevettes

Cooking Time: Roux — 12 minutes
              Gumbo — 16 minutes
Utensils: 4 quart casserole
           4-cup glass measuring cup
Servings: 6

2/3 cup flour ⎫ Roux
2/3 cup oil   ⎭

1-1/2 quarts hot water
2 teaspoons salt
1 teaspoon cayenne pepper
1/2 teaspoon pepper
2 pounds shrimp, raw
    and peeled
1/4 cup green onion tops,
    chopped

1. Mix oil and flour together in a 4-cup measure to make a Roux. Cook on **HIGH 6-7 MINUTES** until dark brown. Follow Roux recipe on page 32 for adding onion, celery, bell pepper, parsley, garlic and onion tops. Transfer Roux to a 4 quart casserole.

2. Add hot water (mix well), salt, pepper and shrimp. Microwave on **HIGH 16 MINUTES.** Stir at 5 minute intervals. Sprinkle onion tops on gumbo before serving over rice. Serve Filé separately.

FILÉ is a powder formerly made by the Choctaw Indian squaws from the leaves of the sassafras tree which grows wild in Louisiana. Squaws would gather the green leaves on small branches and hang them up to dry. When thoroughly dried, they would pound the leaves into a very fine powder with a mortar and pestle made from logs, then pass the powder through a hair sieve. The product which resulted was a dull green powder that was and still is used to thicken liquids. Today, it is usually used for gumbo.

BOUILLABAISSE LOUISIANE

BOUILLABAISSE is a provincial dish made of fish cooked in water or wine, flavored with many seasonings, always including saffron, and tomatoes. It is the fishiest of all fish soups because it is made with a concentrated fish stock. It could be called a stew since it does not have much liquid in it as a soup usually does, but the French refer to it as a soup. In Louisiana, the bouillabaisse is prepared from red fish or snapper, whereas in France, sturgeon or perch is used.

Cooking Time: 23 minutes
Utensils: 3 and 4 quart casseroles
Servings: 6

3 pounds frozen red fish or red snapper fillets
12 frozen medium shrimp
1/2 pint (12) oysters, drained

1. Thaw frozen fish. Trim off ¾ pound fish to be used in stock. Cut fish into 6 portions. Pat dry with paper towel. Thaw shrimp and peel. Set oysters and shrimp aside.

Fish Stock

2. Place fish trimmings, seasonings and water in a 3 quart casserole—follow recipe for Fish Stock on page 54.

2 large cloves garlic, minced
1 teaspoon thyme
1 small bay leaf, crumbled
1/2 teaspoon allspice
2 Tablespoons cooking oil

3. In a small bowl, with back of spoon, crush garlic, thyme, bay leaf and allspice to a smooth paste, then stir in oil. Spread mixture over top of each fillet.

1 cup onion, finely chopped
3 Tablespoons parsley, snipped
3 Tablespoons olive oil

4. Sauté onion and parsley in olive oil on **HIGH 3 MINUTES** in a 4 quart casserole. Place fish on top of onions, cover and cook on **HIGH 2 MINUTES.** Remove fish to make sauce.

(Continued on next Page)

BOUILLABAISSE LOUISIANE (Continued)

1 (16 oz.) can tomatoes,
  drained and chopped
2 cups fish stock
1/4 teaspoon ground
  saffron
1-1/2 teaspoons salt
1/2 teaspoon cayenne pepper
1/4 teaspoon Tabasco
1 teaspoon Worcestershire
  sauce
2 slices lemon

5. Stir in tomatoes, fish stock, saffron, salt, pepper, Tabasco, Worcestershire, lemon (and pureed fish and vegetables from stock if a thicker sauce is desired). Cook on **HIGH 10 MINUTES** until mixture comes to a boil. Add fish fillets, shrimp and oysters. Cover with wax paper. Cook on **HIGH 8 MINUTES** or until shrimp turn pink and oysters have curly edges.

APRIL IN PARIS SOUP/potage printanier de Paris

Cooking Time: 30 minutes
Utensils: 4-cup glass measuring cup
       3 quart casserole
Servings: 4

1 pint chicken stock
1 teaspoon salt
1 medium potato
1 medium onion
1 cucumber
1 celery heart w/leaves
1 tart apple
1 Tablespoon water

1. Bring chicken stock and salt to boil, covered in a 4-cup measure. Peel and chop potato, onion, cucumber, celery and apple. Place in a 3 quart dish with 1 Tablespoon water. Cover and microwave on **HIGH 10 MINUTES** to wilt. Add hot stock and cook on **HIGH 20 MINUTES.** Stir once. Put through a fine sieve or blender until smooth.

1 cup light cream
1 Tablespoon butter
1 scant teaspoon curry
      powder
dash of pepper
chopped chives

2. Return to dish and stir in cream, butter, curry and pepper. Chill thoroughly. Sprinkle with chopped chives.

CAULIFLOWER SOUP/soupe chou-fleur

With Parmesan and/or Romano cheese.

Cooking Time: 50 minutes
Utensil: 5 quart dish
Servings: 8

3 quarts hot water
1 large cauliflower,
    with outer leaves

1. Bring water to boil on **HIGH 15 MINUTES** in a 5 quart dish. While water comes to boil, remove leaves, rinse, and chop them into small pieces. Leave cauliflower whole and soak in salted water.

4 cloves garlic, crushed
1 Tablespoon onion,
    minced
1/4 teaspoon oregano
1 Tablespoon salt

2. To boiling water, add whole cauliflower, chopped leaves, garlic, onion, oregano and salt. Cook until cauliflower is tender on **HIGH 40 MINUTES**. Remove head of cauliflower.

6 oz. package noodles
2 Tablespoons butter or
    olive oil
1/2 cup Parmesan or Romano
    cheese or a combination,
    freshly grated
ground pepper

3. Add noodles and cook on **HIGH 10 MINUTES** or until tender. Add butter or oil and cheese. Check seasonings and add a lot of fresh ground pepper. Cauliflower may be separated into flowerets and added to soup.

BAKED ONION SOUP/soupe à l'oignon

Cooking Time: 3 minutes
Utensil: 2 — 8 oz. glass ramekins
Servings: 2

1 (13 oz.) can Crosse &
    Blackwell onion soup
2 croutets (slices of small
    French bread)
2 slices Swiss cheese
2 Tablespoons Parmesan cheese
2 teaspoons butter

1. Pour onion soup into 2 (8 oz.) ramekins. Float a croutet on top covered with Swiss cheese in each. Sprinkle on Parmesan cheese and top with a pat of butter.

2. Microwave one at a time on **HIGH 1½ MINUTES**, or until cheese bubbles around edges.

ONION SOUP/potage à l'oignon

Cooking Time: 20 minutes
Utensil: 3 quart dish
Servings: 6

3 onions, sliced
    thinly
1/4 cup butter

1. In a 3 quart dish, combine butter and onions. Cover and sauté on **HIGH 10 MINUTES** or until onions are tender, stirring once.

2 (10½ oz.) cans beef
    broth
1 cup hot water
1/2 cup dry white wine
1/4 teaspoon salt
1/4 teaspoon cayenne pepper
1/4 teaspoon white pepper

2. Stir in broth, water, wine, salt and pepper. Microwave covered on **HIGH 10 MINUTES.**

6 slices of French bread,
    toasted
1 cup Muenster or Gruyere
    cheese, grated

3. Float slice of French bread in soup bowl. Top each slice with cheese.

OYSTER AND ARTICHOKE SOUP
potage d'huitres et d'artichauts

Cooking Time: 14 minutes
Utensil: 3 quart casserole
Servings: 6

6 Tablespoons butter, melted
1/2 cup shallots, chopped fine
pinch of thyme
1 bay leaf
1/4 teaspoon cayenne pepper
2 Tablespoons flour

1. In a 3 quart casserole, melt butter. Sauté shallots, thyme, bay leaf and pepper on **HIGH 3 MINUTES.** Add flour and whisk well.

1 (13¾ oz.) can chicken broth
1 pint oysters, drained (reserve liquid)
Liquid from oysters plus 1 extra pint of liquid
1 (14 oz.) can artichoke hearts, drained and chopped
2 teaspoons salt
1/4 teaspoon Tabasco

2. Add broth, oyster water, artichokes, salt and Tabasco. Microwave on **HIGH 6 MINUTES.**

1/2 cup whipping cream
3 sprigs parsley, chopped

3. Add oysters and parsley. Cover with wax paper. Cook on **HIGH 5 MINUTES,** then add whipping cream and serve.

OYSTER SOUP/potage d'huîtres

Cooking Time: 13 minutes
Utensils: 2 quart dish
        8-cup glass measuring cup
Servings: 6

**1-1/2 pints oysters, reserve
½ cup liquid
cayenne pepper
white pepper**

1. Season oysters with pepper and frizzle in their own juice in a 2 quart dish until edges are slightly curled, **3 OR 4 MINUTES ON HIGH.** Set aside.

**6 Tablespoons butter
3 Tablespoons flour
3 Tablespoons onion,
    chopped**

2. Micromelt butter in an 8-cup measure, add flour and onion. Sauté on **HIGH 3 MINUTES,** stir frequently.

**1 (10½ oz.) can cream of
    mushroom soup
1/2 cup oyster liquid
3 cups milk, room
    temperature**

3. Add mushroom soup, oyster liquid and milk. Mix well after each ingredient. Microwave on **HIGH 6 MINUTES,** stir at two minute intervals.

**6 Tablespoons green
    onion tops, chopped
1/2 teaspoon salt**

4. Add drained oysters, salt and onion tops to hot milk mixture. Serve. Reheat in individual bowls on **MEDIUM 2 MINUTES.**

SHRIMP AND CORN CHOWDER
potage de crevettes et de maïs

A delicious meal in itself!

Cooking Time: 36 minutes
Utensil: 5 quart casserole
Servings: 8-10

1/2 pound bacon, fried crisp	1. Fry bacon in microwave. Crumble and set aside. Reserve bacon fat.
3 Tablespoons bacon fat 2 cups onion, chopped fine 1 cup celery and leaves, chopped fine 1/2 cup green bell pepper, chopped fine 1/2 cup carrots, grated 1/2 bay leaf, crumbled	2. Place bacon fat, onion, celery, peppers, carrots and bay leaf in a 5 quart casserole. Sauté on **HIGH 6 MINUTES.** Vegetables may be pureed at this time if you prefer a smooth chowder, but it is not necessary.
2 cups potatoes, diced 1/4 cup water 2 Tablespoons flour 4 cups hot water	3. Stir in potatoes and water. Cover. Cook on **HIGH 5 MINUTES.** Sprinkle flour over mixture and stir in hot water. Cover. Bring to boil on **HIGH 10 MINUTES.**
1 (16½ oz.) can cream style corn 1 (16½ oz.) can whole corn 1 (13 oz.) can low fat evaporated milk 2 pounds medium shrimp, cooked and peeled 1 Tablespoon salt 1/2 teaspoon cayenne pepper 1/2 teaspoon black pepper Tabasco to taste	4. Add corn, milk, shrimp, salt, pepper and Tabasco. Cover and cook on **HIGH 15 MINUTES.** Add crumbled bacon and garnish with chopped parsley, if desired.

TURTLE SOUP/potage de tortue

An old South Louisiana recipe.

Cooking Time: Parboil Turtle — 30 minutes
Soup — 1 hour 22 minutes
Utensils: 3 quart dish
4-cup glass measuring cup
5 quart dish
Servings: 8

3 or 4 pounds turtle meat
1 quart hot water
1 teaspoon salt
1 teaspoon pepper
1 onion, sliced
3 whole cloves stuck into
**   one garlic pod**
4 bay leaves
1 slice lemon

1. Place turtle meat, water, salt, pepper, onion, cloves/garlic, bay leaves and lemon in a 3 quart dish. Cover. Microwave on **HIGH 30 MINUTES** or until turtle meat is tender. Remove meat from bone and mince, strain stock and reserve. Set aside. (This could be done the day before and refrigerated.)

2/3 cup oil
2/3 cup flour

2. Make a Roux with oil and flour. Mix together in a 4-cup measure. Cook on **HIGH 6-7 MINUTES.** Stir.

2 cups onion, chopped
**   fine**
1 cup celery, chopped
**   fine**
4 cloves garlic, minced
1 bunch green onions,
**   chopped**
1/4 cup parsley, chopped

3. Add onion, celery, garlic, onion tops and parsley. Cook on **HIGH 5 MINUTES.** Stir once during cooking time. Now pour Roux into a larger dish (4 or 5 quart).

(Continued on next Page)

TURTLE SOUP (Continued)

1 (28 oz.) can whole
    tomatoes, chopped (drain
    and reserve liquid)
1 (6 oz.) can tomato paste
1 quart turtle stock
4 Tablespoons Worcester-
    shire sauce
1 Tablespoon salt
1 teaspoon cayenne pepper
1 quart hot water
2 slices lemon

6 hard boiled eggs

4. Add tomatoes and paste to Roux. Cook on **HIGH 10 MINUTES.** Add turtle meat, stock, tomato liquid, Worcestershire sauce, salt and pepper. Cover with wax paper. Cook on **HIGH 30 MINUTES.** Stir once. Add water and lemon. Cover and cook on **HIGH 30 MINUTES.**

5. Sieve egg yolks. After serving soup, place one heaping tablespoon of yolk in each bowl.

SPINACH ARTICHOKE SOUP
soupe d'epinards et d'artichauts

Serve along with Corn Beef Brisket.

Cooking Time: 17 minutes
Utensil: 3 quart casserole dish
Servings: 6

2 (10 oz.) packages
    frozen chopped spinach

2 cups strained hot broth
    from Corn Beef Brisket
    (page 118)
(2 cups of chicken stock
    may be substituted)
2 cups hot water
2 beef bouillon cubes or
    2 teaspoons granules
1 (14 oz.) can artichoke
    hearts, drained and
    chopped
1/2 pint sour cream

1. Cook spinach in boxes on **HIGH 7 MINUTES** each. Puncture boxes with knife before cooking.

2. In a 3 quart tureen or casserole, combine spinach, hot broth, hot water, bouillon and artichokes. (Corn Beef broth will provide all the seasoning you need!). Cover and microwave on **HIGH 5 MINUTES** or until broth bubbles. Puree ¼ of the mixture at a time in blender. Return pureed mixture to cooking dish. Stir in sour cream. Cook uncovered on **HIGH 5 MINUTES**.

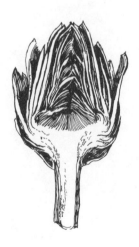

ZUCCHINI SOUP/soupe zucchini

Enticing flavor and a pretty green color!

Cooking Time: 15 minutes
Utensil: 8-cup glass measuring cup
Makes 1¼ quarts

3 chicken bouillon cubes
1 teaspoon curry powder
2-1/2 cups hot water

1. Dissolve the bouillon cubes and curry powder in hot water.

3 medium (about 1 lb.)
zucchini, unpared
and grated
1 large onion, thinly
sliced
2 teaspoons salt
1/4 teaspoon cayenne pepper

2. Place grated zucchini, onion, salt and pepper in an 8-cup measure. Cover. Cook on **HIGH 5 MINUTES.**

   Pour bouillon liquid over zucchini. Cover. Cook on **MEDIUM 10 MINUTES.**

   Puree in an electric blender.

1/2 cup milk

3. Stir in milk. Reheat when ready to serve.

Fish

Shellfish

Fish/Shellfish:
Louisiana, the sportsman's paradise, has the finest fresh water fish in the world in its many lakes, rivers, bayous and swamps. Just a few miles south are the salty bays off the Gulf of Mexico—a true paradise for sport and commercial fishermen.

BAKED FISH FILLETS/poissons au four

Cooking Time: 19 minutes
Utensils: Flat baking dish
4-cup glass measuring cup
Servings: 4

1-1/2 to 2 pounds fish
    fillets
cayenne pepper
1 Tablespoon lemon juice
1/8 teaspoon paprika

1. Season fish with pepper and place in a flat baking dish. Top with lemon juice and paprika.

2 Tablespoons butter
2 Tablespoons flour
1 cup milk
1 teaspoon salt

2. In a 4-cup measure, melt butter on **HIGH 1 MINUTE.** Add flour and salt and stir in milk slowly. Cook on **HIGH 2 OR 3 MINUTES** until thick. Pour sauce over fish.

1/4 cup bread crumbs
1 Tablespoon parlsey,
    chopped

3. Sprinkle on bread crumbs and parsley. Microwave on **MEDIUM 15 MINUTES,** rotate dish at 7 minutes.

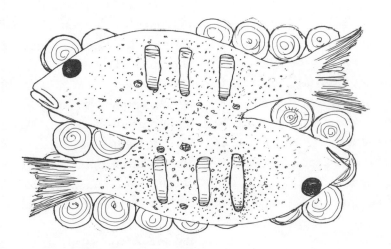

FILLET OF FLOUNDER
WITH SAUCE MEUNIERE
filets de flounder au sauce meuniere

Cooking Time: 6-7 minutes
Utensil: Flat glass baking dish
Servings: 4

4 fillet of flounder,
   (2 lbs.) (bass, red
   fish, red snapper or
   trout may be substituted)

1. Dry fish on paper towels before placing in a glass baking dish.

SAUCE MEUNIERE

1/4 cup butter
1 Tablespoon Worcestershire
1/4 cup green onion tops,
   chopped
2 teaspoons lemon juice
1/2 teaspoon garlic powder
1/2 teaspoon salt
1/4 teaspoon cayenne pepper

2. Combine ingredients for sauce in a 2-cup measure. Cook on **HIGH 1 MINUTE.** Pour sauce over fillets. Cover with wax paper. Cook on **HIGH 5-6 MINUTES** or until fish flakes easily with a fork. Turn dish once.

Garnish with parsley and lemon slices.

FISH STOCK/ fumet de poissons

Cooking Time: 10 minutes
Utensil: 3 quart dish
Makes 3 cups

3/4 pound fish trimmings
1/4 cup onion, chopped
1/4 cup celery and leaves
**   chopped**
1 bay leaf
1/2 teaspoon thyme
1/4 teaspoon salt
1/4 teaspoon pepper
3 cups hot water

1. Place fish along with onion, celery, bay leaf, thyme, salt, pepper and hot water in a 3 quart dish. Cover. Cook on **HIGH 10 MINUTES.** Let sit 10 minutes then strain stock through fine sieve (will keep 2 or 3 days in the refrigerator or frozen).

2. Puree the strained fish and vegetables in the blender or food processor if you want to thicken Bouillabaisse.

RED FISH COURT BOUILLON

Cooking Time: 50 minutes
Utensils: 4-cup glass measure
           5 quart casserole
Servings: 8

Roux (Recipe on page 32)
    2/3 cup oil
    2/3 cup flour

1. Prepare Roux with 2/3 cup oil and 2/3 cup flour. Cook on **HIGH 7 MINUTES** in a 4-cup measure. Follow complete directions for adding vegetables to Roux on page 32. Pour Roux into a 5 quart casserole.

1 (8 oz.) can tomato sauce
1 (6 oz.) can tomato paste

2. Add tomato sauce and paste to hot Roux. Stir until blended.

1 Tablespoon Worcester-
    shire sauce
1/2 lemon, sliced
1 quart hot water

3. Add Worcestershire, lemon and water. Cover. Cook on **HIGH 20 MINUTES,** stir once or twice during cooking.

Season 5 to 6
    pounds of Red Fish
    with your favorite
    seasoning
1/2 teaspoon pepper
1/2 teaspoon cayenne pepper

4. Add seasoned fish and pepper. Cover. Cook on **HIGH 18 MINUTES.**

1 teaspoon salt
chopped onion tops

5. Add salt and sprinkle with onion tops.

RED FISH FILLETS

Cooking Time: 49 minutes
Utensils: 8-cup glass measuring cup
          4 or 5 quart casserole
Servings: 8

2 Tablespoons olive oil
2 cups onions, chopped
1/2 cup celery, chopped
1/4 cup bell pepper,
    chopped

1. Sauté onions, celery, bell pepper and oil in an 8-cup measure on **HIGH 10 MINUTES.**

1/2 cup green onions,
    chopped
2 cloves garlic, minced
1/2 cup parsley, chopped

2. Stir in green onions, garlic and parsley. Sauté on **HIGH 4 MIN-UTES.**

1 (6 oz.) can tomato paste
1/2 lemon sliced thin
2 cups water
2 teaspoons salt
1/2 teaspoon pepper
1/2 teaspoon cayenne pepper
4 or 5 drops Tabasco
    sauce
5 pounds red fish fillets

3. Stir in tomato paste. Cook on **HIGH 10 MINUTES.** Add lemon, water and seasonings. Cover with plastic wrap, cook on **HIGH 10 MINUTES.**

Place fillets, seasoned with cayenne pepper, in a 4 or 5 quart casserole dish. Pour hot sauce over fish. Cover with lid or plastic wrap. Cook on **HIGH 15 MINUTES.**

RED SNAPPER FILLETS IN ARTICHOKE BUTTER

filets de red snapper au beurre d'artichauts

Cooking Time: 11-12 minutes
Utensils: Flat baking dish, 4-cup glass measuring cup
Servings: 6

6 (2-2½ lbs.) red
   snapper fillets

ARTICHOKE BUTTER SAUCE

1/2 cup butter
   Tablespoons green onion
      tops, chopped
2 Tablespoons parsley,
      chopped
3 cloves garlic, minced
1 Tablespoon lemon juice
1 (8 oz.) can sliced
      mushrooms, drained
1 (14 oz.) can artichoke
      hearts, drained and
      sliced
1 teaspoon salt
1/2 teaspoon cayenne pepper

1. Pat fillets dry with paper towels and place in a flat baking dish.

2. In a 4-cup measure, sauté butter, onion tops, parsley and garlic. Microwave on **HIGH 2 MINUTES**. Add lemon juice, mushrooms, artichokes, salt and pepper. Microwave on **HIGH 2 MINUTES** or until mixture heated through.

3. Pour sauce over fillets. Cover with wax paper and cook on **HIGH 7-8* MINUTES** or until fish flakes easily with a fork. Let stand covered 3 minutes.

*Allow 3 minutes cooking time per pound of fish at room temperature.

57

RED SNAPPER LOUISIANE
WITH BUTTER AND WINE SAUCE

Cooking Time: 9 minutes, fish; 2 minutes, sauce
Utensils: Heavy brown paper or flat glass dish
2-cup glass measuring cup
Servings: 4

3-1/2 pound whole red
snapper, cleaned
salt
cayenne pepper
2 Tablespoons melted
butter with
1 teaspoon grated lemon
rind

1. Pat fish dry with paper towels. Season cavity of fish with salt and pepper. Brush fish with butter and lemon and place on a piece of wax paper large enough to enclose it completely.

2 Tablespoons parsley,
finely chopped
3 green onion tops,
finely chopped
1 tomato, peeled and diced

2. Top fish with parsley, onion tops and tomato.

Fold paper over and secure with toothpicks. Place fish diagonally in microwave on heavy brown paper or in a flat glass baking dish. Cook on **HIGH 9 MINUTES** or until fish flakes easily with a fork. Turn fish half way through cooking time.

BUTTER WINE SAUCE

1/2 cup butter
2 Tablespoons green onion
tops, chopped
2 Tablespoons parsley,
finely chopped
1/4 cup sauterne

Mix ingredients in a 2-cup measure. Cook on **HIGH 2 MINUTES.**

Sauce may be served in individual dishes or poured over the fish before serving.

SALMON ON THE HALF SHELL
saumon sur la coquille

Cooking Time: 11 minutes
Utensil: 2 quart dish
Servings: 4

1 (7¾ oz.) can salmon
1 (4 oz.) can sliced
　mushrooms
milk

1. Drain salmon and mushrooms, reserving liquid. Flake salmon. Add enough milk to salmon and mushroom liquid to measure ¾ cup.

2 Tablespoons butter
1/4 cup green bell pepper,
　finely chopped
2 Tablespoons onion,
　finely chopped
2 Tablespoons flour
1/2 teaspoon salt
1/8 teaspoon pepper

2. Melt butter in a 2 quart dish. Sauté green pepper and onion on **HIGH 3 MINUTES** or until tender. Blend in flour. Gradually add salmon liquid mixture, salt and pepper. Cook on **HIGH 4 MINUTES** until thickened.

2 Tablespoons sherry wine
1 Tablespoon lemon juice

3. Stir in sherry wine, lemon juice, flaked salmon and mushrooms. Spoon into 4 sea shells or ramekins.

1 cup coarse bread crumbs
2 Tablespoons butter,
　melted

4. Mix crumbs and butter. Sprinkle over top of salmon and place filled shells in the microwave. Cook on **HIGH 4 MINUTES** until heated through.

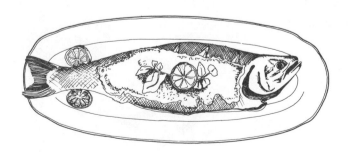

SALMON STUFFED TOMATOES
tomates farcies au saumon

Cooking Time: 12 minutes
Utensils: 2-cup glass measure
    9" glass pie plate
Servings: 6

2 Tablespoons onion,
 finely chopped
2 Tablespoons green bell
 pepper, finely chopped

1. Wilt onions and peppers in a small glass measuring cup on **HIGH 2 MINUTES.** Cover with wax paper.

2 cups (1 pound can) cooked
 salmon, drained
2 eggs, beaten
3/4 cup milk
2 Tablespoons lemon juice
1/2 teaspoon salt
1/4 teaspoon cayenne pepper
1/2 teaspoon Worcestershire
 sauce

2. Mix onions, peppers, salmon, eggs, milk, lemon juice and seasonings together and pour into a 9" pie plate. Cook on **HIGH 8 MINUTES.**

6 medium tomatoes

3. Slice the top off of each tomato, remove the pulp. (This can be used in soups or stews or frozen.) Stuff each tomato with Salmon mixture. Cook on **HIGH 2 OR 3 MINUTES.** Turn dish once. Do not overcook —tomato will split. Garnish with parsley.

This is delicious cold the next day!

CRABMEAT AU GRATIN/crabe au gratin

Cooking Time: 7-8 minutes
Utensils: 8-cup glass measuring cup
        8 sea shells or ramekins
Servings: 8

1/3 cup butter
1 cup onion, chopped fine
1/2 cup celery, chopped
    fine

1. In an 8-cup measure, sauté butter, onion, and celery on **HIGH 3 MINUTES**. Stir once.

3 Tablespoons flour
2 (6 oz.) rolls Kraft
    garlic cheese
1 (4 oz.) can sliced
    mushrooms, drained

2. Stir in flour. Add cheese and mushrooms. Cook on **HIGH 2 OR 3 MINUTES** until cheese is melted.

1 teaspoon salt
1/2 teaspoon cayenne pepper
1/4 teaspoon Tabasco
1 pound claw crabmeat,
    thawed and drained

3. Add seasonings and mix well. Fold in crabmeat.

buttered or seasoned
    bread crumbs
paprika
slivered almonds

4. Spoon mixture into 8 sea shells or ramekins. Sprinkle with bread crumbs, paprika and almonds.

    When ready to serve, place 4 filled shells at a time in the microwave and heat on **HIGH 2 MINUTES**.

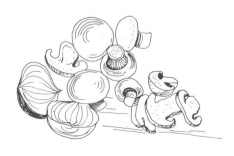

CRABMEAT AUX ARTICHOKES
crabe et artichauts

Cooking Time: 10 minutes
Utensils: 2½ or 3 quart casserole
8-cup glass measuring cup
Servings: 6

**1 pound white lump crab-
meat, thawed
2 (14 oz.) cans artichoke
hearts, drained and diced
4 hard boiled eggs, diced**

**6 Tablespoons butter
1/2 cup flour
2 cups milk
1-1/2 cups grated cheddar
cheese
1 teaspoon salt
1 Tablespoon Worcestershire
sauce
1/2 teaspoon Tabasco
1/4 cup sherry
1/2 cup buttered bread
crumbs**

1. Mix crab, artichokes and eggs together in a 2½ or 3 quart casserole.

2. Micromelt butter in an 8-cup measure. Whisk in flour and add milk gradually. Cook on **HIGH 4 MINUTES**, stirring at 2 minutes. Add cheese, salt, Worcestershire sauce, Tabasco and sherry. Cook on **HIGH 1 MINUTE** until cheese is melted. Fold sauce into crab and artichokes very gently. Top with bread crumbs.

3. Heat through on **HIGH 4-6 MINUTES** until bubbly. Turn dish one time.

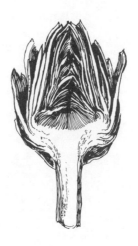

CRABMEAT ÉTOUFFÉE/crabe étouffé

Cooking Time: 27½ minutes
Utensil: 2 quart dish
Servings: 4

3/4 cup butter, melted
2 cups onion, finely
chopped
1/2 cup celery, finely
chopped
1/4 cup green bell pepper,
finely chopped

1. Add onion, celery and bell pepper to melted butter in a 2 quart dish. Sauté on **HIGH 12½ MINUTES.**

1 pound crabmeat
1 teaspoon salt
1/4 teaspoon cayenne pepper
1/2 teaspoon garlic powder
1/2 cup green onion tops,
chopped

2. Add crabmeat, salt, pepper, garlic powder and green onion tops. Cover with wax paper. Cook on **HIGH 10 MINUTES** or until heated through.

1 Tablespoon cornstarch
1 cup hot water

3. For more gravy, pour a mixture of cornstarch and hot water into étouffée. Cook on **HIGH 5 MINUTES.** Serve over hot rice.

CRABMEAT MORNAY IN SHELLS
crabe mornay en coquille

Cooking Time: 12 minutes
Utensil: 2 quart dish
Servings: 6

1/2 cup butter
1/2 pound fresh, or 1 (8 oz.)
 can mushrooms, cut in half
1 small bunch green onions,
 bulbs and tops, chopped
 fine
1/2 cup parsley, chopped fine

1. Micromelt butter 1 minute in a 2 quart measuring cup or dish. Sauté mushrooms, onions and parsley on **HIGH 5 MINUTES.**

2 Tablespoons flour
1-1/2 cups light cream or
 1 (13 oz.) can
 evaporated milk
1/2 pound Swiss cheese,
 grated

2. Blend in flour and cream. Cook on **HIGH 3 MINUTES** or until mixture thickens. Stir in cheese and cook on **HIGH 1 MINUTE** or until cheese is melted.

1 Tablespoon white wine
1 teaspoon salt
1/2 teaspoon cayenne pepper
1 pound white lump crabmeat

3. Add wine, salt and pepper and gently fold in crabmeat.

seasoned bread crumbs

CRAB CASSEROLE MARILYN
crabes casserole mariline

Cooking Time: 12 minutes
Utensils: 10" baking dish
4-cup glass measuring cup
8-cup glass measuring cup
Servings: 6

1 (14 oz.) can artichoke
hearts, drained

1. Slice artichokes and arrange in bottom of a 10" baking dish.

1/2 cup butter
2 bunches green onions, tops
and bulbs — chopped
6 Tablespoons flour
1 cup milk

2. In a 4-cup measure, micromelt butter on **HIGH 1 MINUTE**. Sauté onions on **HIGH 3 MINUTES**. Stir in flour and add milk gradually. Cook on **HIGH 3 MINUTES**. Mixture should be thick.

1 (8 oz.) cream cheese
2 Tablespoons mayonnaise

3. Soften cream cheese in an 8-cup measure on **HIGH 1 MINUTE**. Stir in mayonnaise. Then blend in small amount of white sauce to cream cheese until all is mixed.

1 (8 oz.) can sliced
mushrooms, drained
1 teaspoon salt
1/4 teaspoon white pepper
1/4 teaspoon cayenne pepper
1/2 teaspoon garlic powder
1/4 cup white wine

4. Stir in mushrooms, salt, pepper, garlic powder and wine.

1 pound white lump crabmeat,
drained
seasoned bread crumbs
paprika
1/4 cup sliced almonds

5. Fold crabmeat in gently. Pour over artichokes in baking dish. Sprinkle with bread crumbs, paprika and almonds.

Cook on **HIGH 4 MINUTES** until heated through. Turn dish one time. Serve on toast points, toasted English muffins or in pastry shells.

CRAB CLARICE/crabe clarice

Cooking Time: 16 minutes
Utensil: 3 quart casserole
Servings: 6

1/2 cup butter
2 Tablespoons flour
1/2 cup green onion tops

1. In a 3 quart casserole, melt butter on **HIGH 1 MINUTE.** Stir in flour and onion tops. Sauté on **HIGH 3 MINUTES.** Stir once.

1 (10-¾ oz.) can cream of
    mushroom soup,
    concentrated
1/2 cup milk
1 cup fresh mushrooms,
    sliced
1 teaspoon salt
1/2 teaspoon cayenne pepper
1/4 teaspoon Tabasco

2. Stir in soup, milk, mushrooms, salt, pepper and Tabasco. Microwave on **HIGH 2 MINUTES.**

1 pound white lump crabmeat,
    thawed
1 pound cooked shrimp,
    peeled
1/4 cup pimento, drained
    and chopped
1/4 cup parsley, chopped
seasoned bread crumbs

3. Fold in crabmeat, cooked shrimp, pimento and parsley very gently. Sprinkle bread crumbs over mixture. Cover with wax paper. Cook on **MEDIUM 10 MINUTES.**

CRAB STEW/ragoût de crabe

Cooking Time: Roux — 12 minutes
                  Stew — 30 minutes
Utensils: 4 or 5 quart dish
              4-cup glass measuring cup
Servings: 4-6

2/3 cup oil } **Roux**
2/3 cup flour }

1. Mix oil and flour together in a 4-cup measure to make a Roux. Cook on **HIGH 6-7 MINUTES** until dark brown. Follow Roux recipe on page 32 for adding onion, celery, bell pepper, parsley, garlic and onion tops.

1-1/2 Tablespoons salt
1 teaspoon cayenne pepper
juice of 1/2 lemon
4 cups hot water

2. Pour Roux into a 5 quart dish. Add salt, pepper, lemon juice and water. Cook on **HIGH 10 MINUTES** or until boiling.

2 dozen crabs, cooked
       and cleaned

3. Add crabs. Cover and microwave **20 MINUTES ON HIGH.**

4. Serve in bowls over mounds of white rice.

CRAB VERMILION/crabe vermilion

Try as an appetizer in sea shells.

Cooking Time: 17 minutes
Utensil: 2 quart dish
Servings: 6

4 Tablespoons butter
1/2 pound fresh whole
   mushrooms
3 Tablespoons flour
1 cup chicken stock or bouillon
1/2 cup cream or
   evaporated milk
1/2 teaspoon salt
1/8 teaspoon cayenne pepper
1/8 teaspoon paprika

1. In a 2 quart dish, melt butter and sauté mushrooms on **HIGH 3 MINUTES**. Stir once. Remove mushrooms and set aside. Stir flour into butter. Add chicken stock, cream and seasonings. Cook on **HIGH 6 MINUTES**, stirring every 2 minutes.

1 pound white lump
   crabmeat
1-1/2 Tablespoons sherry
1/2 cup Parmesan cheese,
   grated

2. Fold in crabmeat, mushrooms and sherry. Top with Parmesan cheese. Microwave on **HIGH 8 MINUTES** or until heated through.

STUFFED CRABS/crabes farcis

Cooking Time: 19 minutes
Utensils: 12 crab shells or ramekins
2 quart dish
Servings: 12

1/2 cup butter
1 cup onion, minced
1/2 cup bell pepper, minced
1/2 cup celery, minced
1 clove garlic, minced

1/4 cup green onion tops,
chopped
2 Tablespoons parsley,
chopped
juice of 1/2 lemon

1 teaspoon salt
1/4 teaspoon pepper
1/8 teaspoon cayenne pepper
1/8 teaspoon Tabasco
1/8 teaspoon Worcestershire
sauce
1/4 cup water
2/3 cup bread crumbs
1 pound crabmeat, thawed

12 cleaned crab shells
or ramekins

1. Micromelt butter in a 2 quart dish on **HIGH 1 MINUTE**. Sauté onion, bell pepper, celery and garlic on **HIGH 5 MINUTES**. Stir once or twice.

2. Add onion tops, parsley and lemon juice. Sauté on **HIGH 3 MINUTES**.

3. Add salt, pepper, Tabasco, Worcestershire sauce, water, bread crumbs and crabmeat.

4. Fill crab shells and sprinkle with more bread crumbs. Place 6 shells at a time on serving plate. Microwave on **HIGH 5 MINUTES**. Turn dish one time during cooking time.

69

CRAWFISH ÉTOUFFÉE/écrevisses étouffées

ÉTOUFFÉE is the French word for "smothered." Any meat or seafood can be smothered in a thick sauce to become an étouffée.

Cooking Time: 15 minutes
Utensil: 2 quart dish
Servings: 4

**1/2 cup butter, melted
1-1/2 cups onion, chopped
fine
1/2 cup green bell pepper,
chopped fine
1 clove garlic, minced
2 Tablespoons flour**

1. In a 2 quart dish, melt butter and add onion, bell pepper and garlic. Cover with plastic wrap and microwave on **HIGH 6 TO 7 MINUTES** or until onions are very soft. Stir in flour.

**1 carton crawfish fat — if
not available, substitute
2 heaping Tablespoons un-
diluted cream of celery
soup**

2. Add fat or celery soup (which works very well). Cover and microwave on **HIGH 4 MINUTES.** If using soup, add 3 drops red food coloring.

**1 pound peeled crawfish tails
1-1/2 teaspoons salt
1/2 teaspoon pepper
squeeze of lemon**

3. Add crawfish tails, cover and cook on **HIGH 4 MINUTES.** Season with salt and pepper. Just before serving squeeze a little lemon into the dish. Serve with rice.

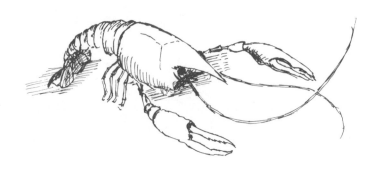

CRAWFISH MONSIGNOR/écrevisses monseigneur

Delicious served in pastry shells or on toast points.

Cooking Time: 14 minutes
Utensils: 2 quart casserole
4-cup glass measuring cup
Servings: 4

1 pound crawfish, peeled
1/2 cup crawfish fat or 1/4
cup butter and 2 Table-
spoons cream of celery
soup — undiluted
1/2 teaspoon cayenne pepper

1. Place crawfish, fat and seasonings in a 2 quart casserole. Cover. Cook on **HIGH 5 MINUTES,** stirring once.

2 Tablespoons butter
2 Tablespoons flour
1/2 cup milk

2. In a 4-cup measure, melt butter, add flour and stir in milk. Blend well, cook on **HIGH 2 MINUTES,** stirring after 1 minute, until mixture thickens.

1 (8 oz.) can sliced
mushrooms, drained
2 Tablespoons green onion
tops, chopped
2 Tablespoons pimento,
chopped
1 teaspoon salt
1/4 teaspoon cayenne pepper
1/4 teaspoon pepper
4 dashes Tabasco Sauce
1/2 cup white wine

3. Stir in mushrooms, onion tops, pimento, seasonings and wine until well blended. Cook on **HIGH 2 MINUTES.** Pour mushroom sauce over crawfish, mix well. Cover. Cook on **MEDIUM 5 MINUTES** before serving over rice.

71

CRAWFISH STEW/ragoût d'écrevisses

Crawfish is a gourmet's delight in Louisiana and a delicacy in France.

Cooking Time: Roux — 12 minutes
Stew — 22 minutes
Utensils: 4-cup glass measuring cup
3 quart dish
Servings: 4-6

2/3 cup oil
2/3 cup flour } Roux

1. Mix oil and flour together in a 4-cup measure. Microwave on **HIGH 6 TO 7 MINUTES.** Follow complete directions for adding vegetables to Roux on page 32. Pour Roux and vegetables into a 3 quart dish.

1 (10 oz.) can Ro-tel
    tomatoes, pureed
2 teaspoons salt
1/4 teaspoon pepper
1/2 teaspoon garlic powder
1 pound peeled crawfish
    tails

2. Add tomatoes, salt, pepper and garlic powder. Cover with plastic wrap. Microwave on **HIGH 12 MINUTES.** Stir 1 or 2 times. Add crawfish, cover and cook on **MEDI-UM 10 MINUTES,** stirring one time.

Serve with rice.

CRAWFISH STUFFED PEPPERS
poivrons farcis aux écrevisses

Shrimp can be substituted.

Cooking Time: 20 minutes
Utensils: 8-cup glass measuring cup
2 round baking dishes
Servings: 8-10

1/2 cup butter
2 cups onion, chopped
fine
1/2 cup bell pepper,
chopped fine
1 cup celery, chopped
4 cloves garlic, minced
2 Tablespoons parsley,
chopped

1. In an 8-cup measure, sauté butter, onion, pepper, celery, garlic and parsley on **HIGH 6 MINUTES.**

1 pound peeled crawfish
tails, cut in half

2. Add crawfish (or shrimp). Cook on **HIGH 4 MINUTES.** After cooking, reserve 10 crawfish for garnish.

1 teaspoon salt
1/2 teaspoon cayenne pepper
1/4 teaspoon Tabasco
1 egg, beaten
1/2 loaf French bread, cut in
bite size pieces

3. Add salt, pepper, Tabasco, egg and French bread that has been soaked in water and squeezed out. Blend well.

4 or 5 medium bell
peppers, halved

4. Cut peppers in half, remove seeds, and place in 2 glass dishes. Cover with wax paper and cook 4 at a time on **HIGH 2 MINUTES.** Spoon crawfish mixture into shells. Cover with wax paper and microwave on **HIGH 3 MINUTES,** turning plate once.

Micro Memo:

Stuffed peppers freeze very well. Place several in plastic bags. Reheat on Medium until warmed through.

OYSTERS BIENVILLE/huîtres bienville

Cooking Time: 16 minutes
Utensils: 1½ quart bowl
        Small glass bowl
        24 oyster shells
        6 soup plates
Servings: 6

2 Tablespoons butter
4 green onions, chop all of
    bulbs and 1/2 of tops
2 Tablespoons flour

1. Melt butter in a 1½ quart bowl. Sauté onions on **HIGH 3 MIN- UTES.** Stir once. Stir in flour and cook on **HIGH 1 MINUTE.**

2/3 cup fish stock, oyster
    or clam juice
1/3 cup drained mushrooms,
    finely chopped
1 egg yolk
1/3 cup dry white wine
1/4 teaspoon salt
1/4 teaspoon white pepper

2. Whisk in stock or juice, add mush- rooms and cook on **HIGH 2 MIN- UTES** until thickened. Stir once. Beat yolk, wine, salt and pepper together and add to sauce. Cook on **HIGH 4 MINUTES.** Stir once.

2 dozen raw oysters,
    drained
6 soup plates filled with
    rock salt or 6 plates
    with a terry towel
    placed on plate
24 oyster shells
1/2 cup seasoned bread
    crumbs
1/2 cup Parmesan cheese
4 Tablespoons butter,
    melted

3. To help drain oysters, place them in a glass bowl and heat on **HIGH 1½ MINUTES.** Drain in a colan- der. Place 4 oyster shells on a plate (if rock salt is used, preheat bowl, rock salt and shells on **HIGH 1 MINUTE**). Place oysters on shells and pour sauce over. Sprinkle with bread crumbs, cheese and butter. Cover with wax paper, place 2 plates at a time in microwave and cook on **HIGH 1½ MINUTES.**

OYSTER COQUILLES/huîtres en coquille

Cooking Time: 20 minutes
Utensils: 2 quart dish
8-cup glass measuring cup
6 or 8 sea shells or ramekins
Servings: 6-8

1/4 cup butter, melted
1/2 pound fresh mushrooms,
sliced or 1 (8 oz.) can
sliced mushrooms, drained
1 cup onion, chopped
2 Tablespoons green onion
tops, chopped
2 Tablespoons parsley,
chopped
1/4 cup white wine
3 dozen raw oysters, drained
and cut in half

1. Sauté butter, mushrooms, onions and parsley in a 2 quart glass dish on **HIGH 8 MINUTES**. Add wine.

Micro Memo: To help remove most of the oyster liquid, place oysters in a glass bowl, and microwave on **HIGH 2 MINUTES,** *drain well.*

1/4 cup butter
2 Tablespoons flour
1/2 cup milk
1 egg beaten
1/2 cup cheddar cheese,
grated
1 teaspoon salt
1/2 teaspoon Tabasco
1/4 teaspoon tarragon

2. In an 8-cup measure, melt butter, blend in flour and stir in milk slowly. Cook on **HIGH 2 MINUTES** or until mixture thickens, stir once. Stir in mushroom sauce, drained oysters, egg, cheese, salt, Tabasco and tarragon. Cover. Microwave on **HIGH 4 MINUTES,** stir once.

1/2 cup buttered bread
crumbs

3. Spoon mixture into sea shells or ramekins. Sprinkle with bread crumbs. When ready to serve, place 4 filled shells at a time in microwave. Cook on **HIGH 3 MINUTES**.

OYSTERS IN A BLANKET/huîtres enveloppées

Cooking Time: 6 minutes
Utensil: 5" x 9" loaf dish
Servings: 6

6 or 8 large slices of
   mushroom
2 Tablespoons chopped
   parsley and chives

1. Place a row of sliced mushrooms the length of a 5" x 9" loaf dish (for decoration). Sprinkle 1 Tablespoon of the parsley and chives mixture over mushrooms.

4 cups cooked rice
1/4 cup butter (reserve
   2 Tablespoons)
1 pint raw oysters,
   (reserve liquid)
1/2 cup evaporated milk
1/2 teaspoon salt
1/4 teaspoon cayenne pepper
1/2 teaspoon Tabasco Sauce

2. Layer dish with 2 cups rice, softened butter, oysters, the remaining parsley and chives, milk, salt, pepper and Tabasco. Cover oysters with the remaining 2 cups rice.

1/2 cup oyster liquid
reserved 2 Tablespoons
   butter

sprigs of parsley

3. Pour butter and oyster liquid over loaf. Cover with wax paper. Cook on **HIGH 6 MINUTES.** Let sit 5 minutes before turning out onto serving plate. Garnish with sprigs of parsley.

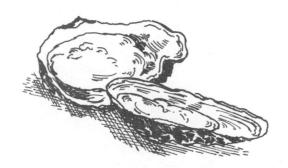

OYSTERS ORLEANS/huîtres à l'Orleans

On the half shell!

Cooking Time: 10 minutes
Utensils: 2 quart bowl
            Oyster shells
Servings: 6

1/2 cup butter, melted
1/4 cup green onion tops,
    chopped fine
1 (4 oz.) can sliced
    mushrooms
1 teaspoon dry mustard
1/4 teaspoon cayenne pepper

1. In a 2 quart bowl, melt butter and sauté onions, mushrooms, mustard and peppers on **HIGH 4 MINUTES.**

3/4 cup flour
2 cups warm milk
1/2 cup dry sherry
1/2 teaspoon salt

2. Stir in flour and add warm milk gradually. Cook on **HIGH 3 OR 4 MINUTES** until sauce thickens. Add sherry and salt.

2 egg yolks, beaten
2 dozen raw oysters,
    drained

3. Stir in beaten egg yolks. Place room temperature raw oysters in oyster shells or larger shells and cover with sauce. Place 6 oyster shells or 4 large shells at a time in mircowave. Cook on **HIGH 2 MINUTES** or until heated through.

OYSTERS ROCKEFELLER

3 dozen

Cooking Time: 27 minutes preparation
1½ minutes per batch
Utensils: 8-cup measuring cup
oyster shells
Servings: 6

2 (10 oz.) packages, frozen chopped spinach
2 teaspoons instant beef bouillon granules

1. Microwave spinach in packages (puncture box with knife) on **HIGH 7 MINUTES EACH.** Rearrange boxes one time. After cooking, open boxes and sprinkle beef bouillon granules on spinach. Set aside.

8 slices bacon, diced
3 cloves garlic, minced

2. Microwave diced bacon covered in an 8-cup measure on **HIGH 5 MINUTES.** Pour off fat and continue cooking on **HIGH 1 OR 2 MINUTES** until bacon is crisp. Remove bacon and add garlic to remaining bacon fat. Saute on **HIGH 1 MINUTE.**

1/4 cup butter
1/2 cup green onion tops, chopped
1/2 cup parsley, finely chopped
1 teaspoon celery salt
1/4 teaspoon cayenne pepper
1/2 cup oyster liquid
1/4 cup (or more) seasoned bread crumbs
3 dozen raw oysters, drained

3. Add butter and green onion tops and sauté on **HIGH 2 MINUTES.** Return bacon, add spinach, parsley, celery salt, pepper and oyster liquid. Thicken with bread crumbs. Cook on **HIGH 3 MINUTES.**

4. Place a terry towel or handi-wipe on a plate and arrange 6 oyster shells in a circle. Top each oyster in its shell with the sauce. Cover with wax paper and microwave on **HIGH 1½ MINUTES.** Have the next plate of 6 ready to slip in the microwave. You will be surprised how long they stay warm.

OYSTER STEW/ragoût de huîtres

Cooking Time: 7 minutes
Utensil: 3 quart dish
Servings: 4-5

4 Tablespoons butter
1/2 teaspoon Worcestershire
sauce
1/2 teaspoon celery salt
1/4 cup green onion tops,
minced
1 pint oysters, drained
(reserve liquid)

1. Place butter, Worcestershire sauce, celery salt, onions and oysters in a 3 quart dish. Microwave on **HIGH 3 MINUTES** until oysters curl around edges.

oyster liquid
1 (13 oz.) can evaporated
milk
1 teaspoon salt
1/4 teaspoon white pepper

2. Add oyster liquid, milk, salt and pepper. Microwave on **HIGH 4 MINUTES.** Stir at 2 minutes.

paprika
sprigs of parsley

3. Sprinkle with paprika and serve with sprigs of parsley.

BARBECUED SHRIMP LAFAYETTE
crevettes en barbecue à la Lafayette

Serve lots of French bread and paper napkins!

Cooking Time: 12-14 minutes
Utensils: 7" x 11" glass dish
          4-cup glass measuring cup
Servings: 4 to 6

3 pounds large shrimp,
    unpeeled
cayenne pepper
black pepper
garlic powder

1. Wash and drain shrimp well. Sprinkle shrimp generously with pepper and garlic and place in a glass dish (approximately 7" x 11").

SAUCE

1 pound (4 sticks) butter
1/3 cup Worcestershire
    sauce
juice of 2 lemons
1/4 teaspoon Tabasco

2. Heat ingredients for sauce in a 4-cup measure on **HIGH 1½-2 MINUTES.** Pour over shrimp. Cover with wax paper. Cook on **HIGH 10-12 MINUTES.** Stir shrimp once or twice during cooking time until all shrimp are pink and tender.

2 teaspoons salt
    (after cooking)

3. Add salt. Let stand 3 minutes. Test for doneness.

    Serve French bread along with shrimp for dipping into hot butter sauce.

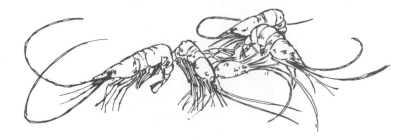

BARBECUED SHRIMP ORLEANS
crevettes en barbecue à l'Orléans

Cooking Time: 12-14 minutes
Utensils: 7" x 11" glass baking dish
4-cup glass measuring cup
Servings: 4 to 6

**3 pounds large shrimp,
unpeeled**

1. Wash and drain shrimp well. Place in a glass baking dish (7" x 11").

SAUCE

**1-1/2 pounds (6 sticks)
butter
3 Tablespoons black pepper
(Fisher's if available)
1 teaspoon cayenne pepper
1 teaspoon accent
1/2 teaspoon paprika
1/8 teaspoon rosemary
1/8 teaspoon thyme
1/8 teaspoon oregano
pinch of cinnamon
2 teaspoons salt
(after cooking)**

2. Place all ingredients for the sauce in a 4-cup measure. Heat on **HIGH 1½-2 MINUTES** or until butter is melted. Pour over shrimp. Cover with wax paper. Cook on **HIGH 10-12 MINUTES.** Stir shrimp once or twice during cooking time until all shrimp are pink. Add salt after cooking. Let stand 3 minutes. Test for doneness.

3. Serve with French bread—perfect for dipping into butter sauce.

Micro Memo:

To reduce recipe: Cooking time for 1½ pounds of shrimp will be approximately 7-8 minutes.

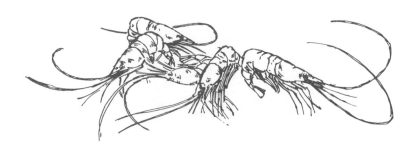

COQUILLES ST. JACQUES

Quick and easy with fish, shrimp and clams!

Cooking Time: 14 minutes
Utensils: 1 quart glass dish
8-cup glass measuring cup
6 sea shells or ramekins
Servings: 6

1 pound frozen flounder fillets
1 pound peeled raw shrimp
1/4 cup water
1/4 cup white wine
1 (4 oz.) can sliced mushrooms, drained
1 (8 oz.) can minced clams, drained
1/2 teaspoon salt
1/4 teaspoon cayenne pepper

1. Cut fish into 1" cubes. Place fish, shrimp, water and wine in a glass bowl. Cover and cook on **HIGH 5 MINUTES** or until shrimp are pink, stirring once. Drain. Add mushrooms, clams, salt and pepper.

1 (10-¾ oz.) can cream of potato soup, pressed through a sieve
1/2 cup sour cream
1/2 cup Parmesan cheese

2. In an 8-cup measure, mix pureed potato soup, sour cream and ½ of the Parmesan cheese. Microwave on **HIGH 3 MINUTES.** Fold in fish mixture. Spoon into 6 sea shells or ramekins and sprinkle with remaining cheese. Place 3 filled shells at a time in the microwave. Cook on **MEDIUM 3 MINUTES** or until heated through.

SHRIMP A LA CREOLE/crevettes créoles

Cooking Time: 36 minutes
Utensil: 3 quart dish
Servings: 6

1-1/2 cups celery, chopped
1-1/2 cups onion, chopped
1/2 cup green onions,
  chopped
3 cloves garlic, minced
1/2 cup bell pepper,
  chopped
4 Tablespoons oil
1 Tablespoon flour

1. In a 3 quart dish, sauté celery, onion, green onions, garlic and bell pepper in oil on **HIGH 20 MIN-UTES.** Cover with wax paper or plastic wrap. Cook until all are wilted. Stir in flour.

1 (10 oz.) can Ro-tel tomatoes
  and green chilies, chopped
1 (8 oz.) can tomato sauce
1 (13-¾ oz.) can chicken
  or beef broth
2 pounds raw medium shrimp,
  peeled
1 teaspoon salt

2. Add tomatoes, sauce and broth. Bring to a boil on **HIGH 10 MIN-UTES.** Add shrimp, cover with wax paper. Microwave on **HIGH 6 MINUTES** or until shrimp are pink and tender. Stir once or twice. Add salt and let stand 5 minutes.

Micro Memo:

Allow 5 minutes sautéing time per cup of fresh chopped vegetables such as onions, green peppers, and celery. Always heat butter or oil before adding vegetables.
Sautéing time will be shorter for vegetables in a hot Roux.

SHRIMP AND CRABMEAT CASSEROLE
crevettes et crabe casserole

Cooking Time: 8-10 minutes
Utensils: 3 quart casserole
2-cup glass measuring cup
Servings: 8

1 pound cooked shrimp,
peeled
1 pound white lump
crabmeat
1 cup mayonnaise
1/2 cup green bell pepper,
chopped
1/2 cup onion, chopped
1/2 cup celery, chopped
1/2 teaspoon salt
1/4 teaspoon pepper
1 teaspoon Worcestershire
sauce
1 teaspoon paprika

1/2 cup seasoned or
buttered bread crumbs

1. Cook shrimp in the microwave—see directions on page 28.

2. Place bell pepper, onion and celery in a 2-cup measure. Cover with wax paper and cook on **HIGH 2 MINUTES** until just wilted.

3. Combine all ingredients in a 3 quart casserole.

4. Sprinkle top with bread crumbs. When ready to serve, heat through on **HIGH 6-8 MINUTES.** Turn dish once.

84

SHRIMP AND SHELLS/crevettes et coquilles

Cooking Time: 8 minutes
Utensils: 3 quart casserole
4-cup glass measuring cup
Servings: 6 to 8

2 cups cooked, small macaroni shells
2 cups cooked shrimp, peeled (small to medium size)

1. Place shells and shrimp in a 3 quart casserole.

1/2 cup onion, chopped
2 Tablespoons parsley, chopped
2 Tablespoons butter

2. In a 4-cup measure, sauté onion and parsley in butter on **HIGH 3 MINUTES.**

1 (10 oz.) can cream mushroom soup, concentrated
1/2 can milk
1 (4 oz.) can sliced mushrooms, drained
1 cup cheddar cheese, grated
1/2 teaspoon salt
1/4 teaspoon cayenne pepper

3. Add soup, milk, mushrooms, half of the cheese, salt and pepper to onions and parsley. Pour over shrimp and shells.

1/4 cup bread crumbs

4. Top with remaining cheese and bread crumbs. Cook on **HIGH 5 MINUTES** or until heated through.

SHRIMP ÉTOUFFÉE/crevettes étouffées

Cooking Time: 28 minutes
Utensil: 2 quart dish
Servings: 4

1/2 cup butter, melted
1-1/2 cups onion, chopped
1/2 cup green bell pepper,
   chopped
1/2 cup celery, chopped
3 cloves garlic, minced

1. In a 2 quart dish, melt butter and sauté onion, pepper, celery and garlic on **HIGH 15 MINUTES**, covered.

2 Tablespoons flour
1/2 cup Bloody Mary Mix
2 heaping Tablespoons
   undiluted cream of
   celery soup
1 teaspoon salt

2. Stir in flour and Bloody Mary Mix. Add cream of celery soup and salt. Cover. Microwave on **HIGH 5 MINUTES**.

1 pound raw shrimp,
   peeled
1/2 teaspoon cayenne pepper
1/8 teaspoon Tabasco
lemon juice

3. Add shrimp, pepper and Tabasco. Microwave on **HIGH 8 MINUTES** or until shrimp are pink and tender. Stir once or twice. Squeeze a small amount of lemon juice over étouffée and serve with rice.

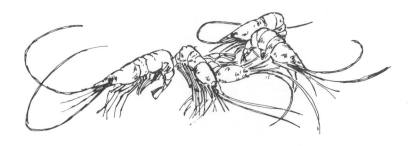

SHRIMP, NATURALLY!

Cooking Time: 12 minutes
Utensil: 2 quart casserole
Servings: 4

1/2 cup butter, melted
1 cup onion, chopped
2 cloves garlic, minced

1. In a 2 quart casserole, melt butter and add onion and garlic. Microwave on **HIGH 5 MINUTES** or until onion is tender.

1 teaspoon Worcestershire sauce
1 teaspoon salt
1/2 teaspoon Tabasco
2 pounds peeled raw shrimp
2 Tablespoons parsley, minced
2 Tablespoons green onion tops, minced

2. Add Worcestershire, salt, Tabasco and shrimp. Stir to mix well. Cover with wax paper and microwave on **HIGH 4 MINUTES.** Stir. Cook on **HIGH 3 MINUTES** or until all shrimp are pink. Add parsley and onion tops after cooking. Taste to adjust seasonings. Serve alongside rice.

SHRIMP THERMIDOR/crevettes thermidor

Cooking Time: 8 minutes
Utensil: 3 quart casserole
Servings: 6-8

1 pound medium shrimp, peeled and cooked

Recipe for Steamed Shrimp is on page 28.

5 slices white bread
1/4 cup butter, softened

1. Remove crust from bread. Soften butter 10 seconds, spread generously on bread and cut into ½" cubes.

2 cups cheddar cheese, grated

2. In a 3 quart casserole, layer ½ of bread, ½ of shrimp and then ½ of the cheese. Repeat layers.

3 eggs, beaten slightly
1-1/2 cups milk
1/2 teaspoon salt
1/4 teaspoon cayenne pepper

3. In a small mixing bowl, combine eggs, milk, salt and pepper. Pour over contents in casserole. Cover and microwave on **HIGH 8 MINUTES.**

SHRIMP OLIVER/crevettes oliver

Cooking Time: 11 minutes
Utensil: 2 quart dish
Servings: 4

1/4 cup butter, melted
2 Tablespoons onion,
    finely chopped
3 cloves garlic, minced
1 pound raw shrimp,
    peeled
1 Tablespoon parsley,
    chopped
dash of paprika
1/4 teaspoon Tabasco
1/4 teaspoon cayenne pepper

1. Melt butter in a 2 quart dish. Sauté onion and garlic on **HIGH 2 MINUTES**. Add shrimp, parsley, paprika, Tabasco and pepper. Cover. Cook on **HIGH 7 MINUTES** or until shrimp are pink and tender. Stir once or twice.

1 Tablespoon flour
1 Tablespoon water
2 Tablespoons white wine
1-1/2 teaspoons salt

2. Stir in flour, water, wine and salt. Cook on **HIGH 2 MINUTES** or until mixture thickens.

Cooked egg noodles

3. Serve over medium egg noodles that have been tossed with butter and Parmesan cheese.

SHRIMP STEW/ragoût de crevettes

Cooking Time: Roux — 12 minutes
Stew — 19 minutes
Utensils: 4-cup glass measuring cup
3 quart dish
Servings: 4-6

2/3 cup flour ⎫
2/3 cup oil ⎬ Roux (page 32)

1. Make a Roux with oil and flour in a 4-cup measure. Microwave on **HIGH 6 TO 7 MINUTES,** stirring at 6 minutes. See recipe on page 32 for adding vegetables. Transfer Roux and vegetables to a 3 quart dish.

1/2 cup hot water
1 (10 oz.) can Ro-tel
tomatoes and peppers,
pureed
2 teaspoons salt
1/4 teaspoon pepper
1 pound raw shrimp,
peeled

2. Add hot water, tomatoes and liquid, salt and pepper. Cover with lid or plastic wrap. Microwave on **HIGH 12 MINUTES.** Add shrimp, cover and cook on **HIGH 7 MINUTES** until shrimp are pink and tender. Stir 2 times. Serve with cooked rice.

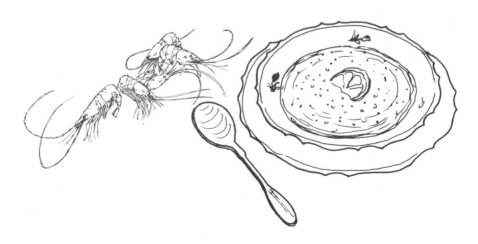

BAKED SEAFOOD SALAD

Cooking Time: 11 minutes
Utensil: 3 quart dish
Servings: 8

4 Tablespoons butter
1 (8 oz.) can sliced
    mushrooms, drained
3/4 cup green peppers,
    chopped
1/2 cup onion, chopped

1 (8 oz.) can water
    chestnuts, sliced thin
2-1/2 cups mayonnaise
1 teaspoon creole mustard
1-1/2 teaspoons salt
1/2 teaspoon cayenne pepper
2 teaspoons Worcestershire
    sauce
4 hard cooked eggs, chopped
2 cups celery, finely
    chopped
1 pound cooked shrimp,
    small and peeled
1 pound white lump
    crabmeat
2 cups buttered bread
    crumbs
paprika

1. In a 2½ or 3 quart dish, sauté butter, mushrooms, green peppers and onion on **HIGH 3 MINUTES.**

2. Stir in water chestnuts, mayonnaise, mustard, salt, pepper, Worcestershire Sauce, eggs and celery. Fold in shrimp and crab. Sprinkle with bread crumbs and paprika. Cover with wax paper. Microwave on **HIGH 8 MINUTES** until heated through. Let stand 5 minutes.

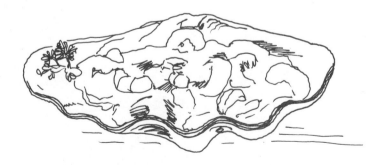

STEAMED LOBSTER TAILS/langoustes étuvées

Cooking Time: 10 minutes
Utensil: 1 quart dish
Servings: 3-4

3 large or 4 small lobster tails (3 oz. each)
1-1/2 cups water
1 slice lemon
1 teaspoon salt

1. Place lobster tails in a 1 quart casserole. Arrange so meaty portion is near outer edge of dish. Add water, lemon and salt. Cover. Cook on **HIGH 10 MINUTES,** or until tails are a bright pink color. Let stand in dish a few minutes.

Melted butter
Lemon wedges

2. Loosen by running knife between shell and meat. Serve with melted butter and lemon.

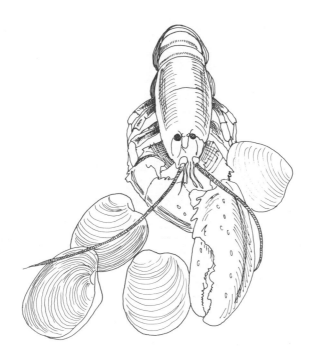

Poultry/Game

Poultry:
   Poultry cooked in the microwave is always tender and moist. You will find an interesting variety of recipes in this section.

POULTRY

Game:
   Wild game in Louisiana is as abundant as are the recipes. The microwave enables one to serve the hunter's delight in a fraction of the conventional cooking time.

GAME

BAKED CHICKEN IN LEMON & SOY SAUCE
poulet au four à la sauce de soja et de citron

Cooking Time: 18 minutes
Utensil: 10" glass dish
Servings: 4

3 lb. chicken

1. Cut chicken into pieces and place in dish.

1/4 cup soy sauce
3 lemons, cut in wedges
1/4 cup butter, melted
1/4 teaspoon onion salt
1 cup water
1 teaspoon paprika

2. Mix together soy sauce, lemon wedges, butter, onion salt, water and paprika. Coat chicken with this mixture. Cover and cook on **HIGH 18 MINUTES.** Turn dish once or twice.

3. Allow 10 minutes standing time.

BARBECUED CHICKEN/poulet en barbecue

Cooking Time: 42 minutes
Utensils: Flat glass baking dish
4-cup measuring cup
Servings: 6

3 pound fryer, cut up
1/4 teaspoon cayenne pepper
1 onion, sliced
1/2 lemon, sliced

1. Season chicken with cayenne pepper and place in baking dish. Arrange chicken so that the meaty portions are near the outer edge of dish and boney portions in the center. Place sliced onion and lemon on top of chicken. Cover with wax paper and microwave on **HIGH 8 MINUTES.** Turn dish at 4 minutes.

SAUCE

1/4 cup Worcestershire
sauce
1/2 cup catsup
1/2 cup water
1/2 teaspoon Tabasco
1 teaspoon salt
1 teaspoon chili powder
1/2 teaspoon garlic powder

2. Mix Worcestershire sauce, catsup, water, Tabasco, salt, chili powder and garlic powder in a 4-cup measure and microwave on **HIGH 3 OR 4 MINUTES** until sauce comes to boil. Pour sauce over chicken, cover with wax paper and microwave on **HIGH 30 MINUTES** or until chicken is done. Turn dish every 10 minutes.

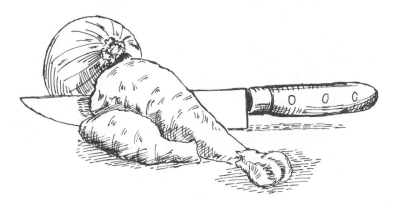

CHICKEN AU VIN/poulet au vin

Cooking Time: 16-18 minutes
Utensil: 12" glass dish
Servings: 4

1 (10 oz.) can cream of mushroom soup
1 (10 oz.) can cream of chicken soup
1 package dry onion soup mix
1 scant cup white wine

2-1/2-3 pound chicken, cut up in pieces

1. Combine mushroom soup, chicken soup and onion soup (all undiluted). Add wine and coat chicken with sauce.

2. Place chicken in a glass dish. Cover with wax paper. Cook on **HIGH 16-18 MINUTES,** or until chicken is tender. Rotate dish at 10 minutes.

3. Allow standing time of 10 minutes.

CHICKEN LIVERS AND AVOCADO IN SOUR CREAM/foies de volaille et avocat au fromage blanc

Cooking Time: 12 minutes
Utensil: 3 quart casserole
Servings: 6

1/2 cup butter
1 cup onion, chopped
1/2 lb. mushrooms,
    sliced
1 lb. chicken livers

1. Melt butter in casserole dish. Sauté livers, onions, mushrooms for **10 MINUTES ON HIGH,** stirring every 3-4 minutes.

2 avocados, sliced
2 Tablespoons lemon juice
1 Tablespoon Worcestershire
    sauce
1/2 teaspoon pepper
1 teaspoon salt
1 Tablespoon paprika

2. Sprinkle avocados with lemon juice, Worcestershire sauce, pepper, salt and paprika. Add avocados to livers and cook on **HIGH 2 MINUTES.**

1 cup sour cream

3. Fold in sour cream. Serve over toast or rice.

CHICKEN 'N' CHILIES

Cooking Time: 8 minutes
Utensil: 2 quart casserole
Servings: 6-8

1 can (10-¾ oz.) cream
   of chicken soup
1 can (4 oz.) green chilies,
   diced
1/4 teaspoon instant minced
   onion
1/2 cup water

1. In a small mixing bowl, place soup, chilies, onion and water. Stir until well blended.

2 large, firm ripe
   tomatoes

2. Peel tomatoes and slice thin.

1 package (6 oz.) corn
   chips
2 cans (5 oz. each) boned
   chicken, diced
1 cup shredded mild
   cheddar cheese

3. In a 2 quart casserole, layer ½ of corn chips, 1 can diced chicken, ½ of tomato slices, ½ of soup mixture, then sprinkle with half of cheese. Repeat layers in same order, ending with cheese. Cook uncovered on **HIGH 8 MINUTES.**

CHICKEN ORIN/poulet orin

Cooking Time: 25 minutes
Utensil: 10″ baking dish
Servings: 6

1 package (6 oz.) Uncle Ben's
    Wild Rice and Mix
1 (10-¾ oz.) can cream of
    mushroom soup
3/4 cup hot water
1 (16 oz.) can Chinese
    Vegetables, drained

1. In a 10″ baking dish, mix together rice and mix, soup and water. Gently fold in drained vegetables. Cover with wax paper. Cook on HIGH 5 MINUTES. Stir.

4 chicken breasts,
    halved and skinned, or a
    2½ pound chicken, cut up
    and skinned
Soy sauce

2. Place chicken on top of rice mixture. Put a small amount of soy sauce on each piece of chicken. Cover with lid or wax paper. Microwave on HIGH 10 MINUTES. Turn chicken pieces over. Cover and continue to cook on HIGH 10 MINUTES or until chicken is tender.

CHICKEN PARMESAN

Cooking Time: 25 minutes
Utensil: 2 quart flat dish
Servings: 6

2-1/2 pound chicken, cut up
cayenne pepper
onion powder
garlic powder

1. Wash and pat chicken dry with paper towels. Season chicken with pepper, onion and garlic powder.

1/2 cup Parmesan cheese, grated
2 cups seasoned bread crumbs
2 eggs, well beaten with 2 Tablespoons milk

2. Mix parmesan cheese and bread crumbs in a flat dish. Place egg mixture in a flat dish. Dip chicken in egg mixture, then in bread crumb mixture.

1/4 cup butter, melted

3. Arrange chicken in a 2 quart flat dish with meaty portions toward outside of dish and boney portions toward the center. Pour butter over chicken and sprinkle on any remaining crumbs. Cover with wax paper and cook on **HIGH 25 MINUTES.** Rotate dish 2 times.

salt to taste

Salt may be added after cooking.

CHICKEN SPAGHETTI/spaghetti au poulet

Cooking Time: 45 minutes
Utensils: 2 quart dish
         3 quart dish
Servings: 6

2-1/2 pound chicken, cut up
1 cup water
1/2 teaspoon cayenne pepper
1/4 teaspoon pepper
1/4 cup oil
3/4 cup onion, chopped
1/2 cup celery, chopped
1/4 cup bell pepper,
    chopped

1. Season chicken with pepper. Add water and place in a 2 quart dish skin side down with meaty portions to the outside of dish and boney portions toward center of dish. Cover with wax paper. Cook on **HIGH 10 MINUTES**. Turn dish. Cook on **HIGH 10 MORE MINUTES**. Set chicken and stock aside. In a 3 quart dish, sauté onion, celery, and bell pepper in oil on **HIGH 3 MINUTES**.

2 cloves garlic, minced
1/4 cup parsley, chopped
1/4 cup green onion,
    chopped
1 can tomato paste
1/8 teaspoon sugar

2. Add garlic, parsley and green onion. Sauté on **HIGH 2 MINUTES**. Stir in tomato paste and sugar. Microwave on **HIGH 5 MINUTES**. Stir once or twice.

2 cups hot water
1 package spaghetti sauce
    mix with mushrooms
1-1/2 teaspoons salt
1/2 teaspoon cayenne pepper
1/2 cup chicken stock from
    baking dish
1/4 teaspoon hot pepper
    sauce

3. Add water, sauce mix, salt, pepper, chicken stock, hot pepper sauce and chicken pieces. Cover with wax paper. Cook on **HIGH 15 MINUTES** until heated through. Serve over spaghetti or cooked rice.

CHICKEN STEW/ragoût de poulet

Cooking Time: 36 minutes
Utensils: 4-cup measuring cup
3 quart casserole
Servings: 6-8

**2-1/2 to 3 pound chicken,
cut up and cooked
(see page 104)**

2/3 cup flour } Roux
2/3 cup oil

**2 cups onions, chopped
1 cup celery, chopped
1/4 cup green onion,
chopped
1/4 cup parsley, chopped
4 cloves garlic, minced**

**1 cup chicken stock
2 cups hot water
2 teaspoons salt
1/2 teaspoon pepper
1/2 teaspoon cayenne pepper**

1. Cook chicken, set aside and reserve stock. Chicken may be left on the bone or boned for the stew.

2. In a 4-cup measure, mix flour and oil. Cook on **HIGH 6 TO 7 MINUTES.** Stir.

3. Add onions and celery. Sauté on **HIGH 3 MINUTES.** Add green onions, parsley and garlic. Sauté on **HIGH 2 MINUTES.** Pour into 3 quart casserole.

4. Stir in stock, water, seasonings and chicken. Cover. Cook on **HIGH 5 MINUTES.** Stir. Cook on **MEDIUM 20 MINUTES.**

5. Serve over rice.

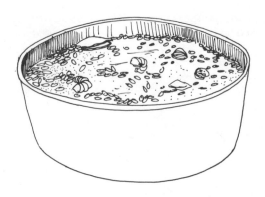

CHICKEN TETRAZZINI/poulet tetrazzini

Cooking Time: 60 minutes
Utensils: 3 quart casserole
5 quart casserole
Servings: 8

**3 pound chicken, cooked and
cut in bite size pieces**
1 teaspoon salt
1 rib celery, cut up
2 small whole onions
**8 oz. spaghetti, broken
in half**

1. Cut chicken up and place in a 3 quart dish with 4 cups hot water, salt, celery and onion. Cover. Microwave on **HIGH 30 MINUTES**. Remove chicken, celery and onion and cook spaghetti in broth. Cook on **HIGH 8 MINUTES**. Stir one time and set aside covered.

1/2 cup butter, melted
**1/2 cup green bell pepper,
chopped**
1 cup onion, chopped
**1 (8 oz.) can sliced
mushrooms**
1/2 cup flour
1-1/2 teaspoons salt
1/2 teaspoon cayenne pepper
2 cups milk, heated
**8 oz. American cheese,
cut up**
**8 oz. sharp cheddar
cheese, cut up**

2. In a 5 quart casserole, melt butter on **HIGH 1 MINUTE**. Sauté bell pepper and onion covered on **HIGH 10 MINUTES**. Stir at 5 minutes. Add mushrooms. Stir in flour, seasonings and add milk gradually. Microwave on **HIGH 2 MINUTES**. Stir in cheese until melted.

3. Add chicken and spaghetti to cheese sauce. Mix well but lightly. Before serving, heat through on **HIGH 9 MINUTES**.

"COOKED" CHICKEN/poulet poche

Cooking Time: 20 minutes
Utensil: 3 quart casserole
Yields: 2 cups boned chicken
and 3 cups stock

Prepare chicken, reserve stock, bone chicken and use in any recipe calling for "cooked chicken." Keep in refrigerator or freezer until ready to use.

2-1/2 to 3 pound chicken
1/2 onion, sliced
1 rib celery and leaves,
cut into pieces
2 cups hot water
1 teaspoon salt
1/2 teaspoon cayenne pepper
1/4 cup white wine

Place chicken, onion, celery, wine, water and seasonings in a 3 quart casserole. Cover. Cook on **HIGH 20 MINUTES.**

CRUNCHY CHICKEN/poulet croûstillant

Cooking Time: 32 minutes
Utensil: 2 quart baking dish
Servings: 4-6

1 clove garlic, minced
1/2 cup butter, melted

1. Sauté garlic and butter in a 2 quart baking dish for **2 MINUTES ON HIGH.**

1 Tablespoon parsley,
   minced
1 teaspoon salt
1/4 teaspoon cayenne pepper
1/4 teaspoon onion powder
1/4 teaspoon black pepper
1 cup dry bread crumbs
3 pound chicken, cut up

2. Combine parsley, salt, pepper, onion powder and bread crumbs in a flat dish.

3. Dip chicken in garlic butter, then in bread crumb mixture. Arrange chicken pieces in the 2 quart baking dish with meaty portions toward outside of dish and boney pieces toward the center. Sprinkle on any remaining crumbs. Cover with wax paper. Microwave on **HIGH 15 MINUTES.** Turn chicken pieces over and continue cooking on **HIGH 15 MINUTES** or until tender. Let stand 5 minutes.

QUICK CHICKEN STOCK/fond de volaille

Cooking Time: 5 minutes
Utensil: 8-cup glass measuring cup
Makes 3 cups

3 cups canned chicken
    broth
1/3 cup vermouth
1 teaspoon celery salt
1 teaspoon onion salt
1 teaspoon Tony's seasoning
    (or your favorite)
1 bay leaf
3 cloves
1 teaspoon tarragon
2 sprigs parsley

Mix all the ingredients together in an 8-cup measure and microwave on **HIGH 5 MINUTES,** or until heated through.

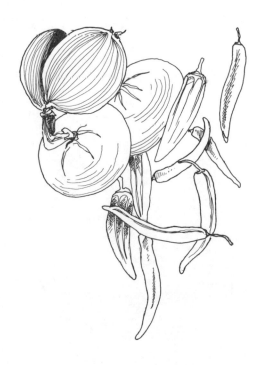

DOVES AND MUSHROOMS
colombe aux champignons

Smothered and tender

Cooking Time: 39 minutes
Utensil: Browning dish and cover
Servings: 4 to 6

12 doves, cleaned
salt and cayenne pepper
garlic powder
bacon fat

1. Season doves inside and outside with pepper and garlic powder. Rub a small amount of bacon fat on breast.

2. Preheat browning dish **4 MINUTES ON HIGH.** Brown doves, turning each one several times in browning skillet. Cover. Cook on **HIGH 9 MINUTES.** Stir and rearrange doves one or two times during cooking time.

2 cups of Roux or
 ½ of recipe
  See page 32
1 (8 oz.) can mushrooms,
 drained
1 teaspoon salt
1/4 teaspoon cayenne pepper
1/4 teaspoon pepper sauce

3. Add mushrooms and seasonings to Roux. Pour over doves. Arrange doves so that the breast is covered with Roux. Cover. Cook on **HIGH 30 MINUTES** or until dove is tender. Baste 2 times during cooking time.

Serve with rice.

DUCK A LA LOUISIANE/canard de Louisiane

Smothered in Roux and mushrooms

Cooking Time: 40 minutes
Utensils: Browning skillet with cover
4-cup glass measuring cup
Servings: 4

4 wild ducks
salt, pepper
cayenne pepper

1 bunch parsley
1 onion, quartered

1/2 of Roux recipe
See Page 32
1 (8 oz.) can mushrooms,
liquid, stems and
pieces

1. Clean duck, season inside with salt and cayenne pepper—and outside with red and black pepper. Divide one bunch of parsley and place a handful in the cavity of each duck, followed with a quarter piece of onion. (This should remove any wild flavor).

2. If you make 1 recipe of Roux, freeze ½ of it in a glass jar for your next recipe calling for Roux. Add mushrooms and liquid to the Roux in a 4-cup measure.

3. Preheat browning skillet for 4 minutes. Place all 4 ducks in the skillet to brown, turning each one several times. Cover and cook on **HIGH 8 MINUTES.** Turn ducks in the skillet one time.

4. Heat Roux and mushrooms on **HIGH 2 MINUTES.** Pour over ducks. Cover. Cook on **HIGH 30 MINUTES** or until ducks are tender. Cut ducks in half with poultry shears and remove parsley and onion before serving.

Cooked rice is perfect with the dark Roux gravy.

Micro Memo:

Allow 9 minutes cooking time per pound of duck.

6 QUAIL IN WINE SAUCE
caille au four dans une sauce au vin

8 doves may be subsituted.

Cooking Time: 33 minutes
Utensil: 10" glass skillet or 3 quart dish
Servings: 6

1/4 cup butter
1/2 cup onion, chopped
1/2 cup celery, chopped
1/2 cup green bell pepper,
   chopped

1. Melt butter in a 10" Corning skillet or a 3 quart casserole on **HIGH 1 MINUTE**. Sauté onion, celery and bell pepper in butter on **HIGH 2 MINUTES**.

6 quail or 8 dove
   (seasoned with black
   pepper, cayenne pepper,
   and paprika)
1 Tablespoon flour
1 cup chicken or beef
   bouillon
3 Tablespoons red wine
1 teaspoon salt

2. Stuff each cavity with a spoonful of sauteed vegetables and place quail, breast down, in dish with remaining vegetables and butter. Cover with lid or wax paper. Microwave on **HIGH 10 MINUTES**. Turn quail over. Stir in flour. Add bouillon, wine and salt. Baste quail. Microwave on **HIGH 15 MINUTES**.

1 (4 oz.) can sliced mushrooms
   and liquid

3. Spoon mushrooms over quail (helps browning). Sprinkle on more paprika. Microwave on **HIGH 5 MINUTES**.

RABBIT SAUCE PIQUANTE/lapin a la sauce piquante

Cooking Time: 52 minutes
Utensils: Browning skillet
5 quart dish
Servings: 6-8

**2 wild rabbits, 3½ pounds,
cut in serving pieces**

1. Preheat browning skillet 4 minutes. Sear rabbit on all sides. Cover and cook on **HIGH 3 MINUTES.** Preheat 2 minutes for additional browning. Set rabbit aside covered in browning dish.

**2 Tablespoons butter,
melted
2 cups onion, chopped
3 cloves garlic, minced
1 (6 oz.) can tomato paste
3 Tablespoons flour
1-1/2 cups hot water**

2. Melt butter in a 5 quart casserole. Sauté onion and garlic on **HIGH 8 MINUTES** or until onion is tender. Add tomato paste, flour and water. Cook on **HIGH 2 MINUTES.**

**1 (10 oz.) can Ro-tel
tomatoes and peppers,
pureed
1 Tablespoon salt
1-1/2 cups sherry
1/2 cup parsley, chopped
1/2 cup green onion tops,
chopped**

3. Add Ro-tel tomatoes and liquid, salt, sherry, rabbit, parsley and onion tops. Cover with wax paper or lid and microwave on **HIGH 36 MINUTES.** Stir every 10 minutes. Serve with rice.

Micro Memo:

Allow 9 minutes cooking time per pound of rabbit.

VENISON ROAST/venaison

Cooking Time: 35 minutes
Utensils: Rack and a glass dish
Servings: 4-6

Venison ham or roast,
    2-3 pounds defrosted
garlic powder
cayenne pepper
black pepper
Worcestershire sauce
Liquid Smoke

2 strips of bacon
salt
2 Tablespoons flour
1/4 cup red wine
1 (4 oz.) can sliced
    mushrooms
1 Tablespoon green onion

1. Cut small pockets in venison and stuff with a paste made of garlic powder, cayenne, black pepper and Worcestershire (proportions according to your taste). Coat roast with Liquid Smoke and sprinkle on seasonings.

2. Cover with wax paper and place on microsafe rack or trivet in a glass dish. Cook on **HIGH 15 MINUTES.** Turn meat over. Place bacon on meat, cover and cook on **HIGH 15 MINUTES.** Remove meat, sprinkle with salt, wrap in foil to retain heat. To make a sauce with remaining liquid, stir in flour, wine, mushrooms and onions. Microwave on **HIGH 3-5 MINUTES.** Sauce may be poured over venison or served separately.

Micro Memo:

Internal temperature should be 170° (well done) after a 10 minute standing time. Reduce cooking time for (medium) — 160°.

Meat

Meat:
   The Microwave can simmer less tender cuts of beef and make them delicious. Pork, veal and tender cuts of beef all cook well and quickly!

BAYOU BOULETS
"Meatballs"

Cooking Time: 14 minutes
Utensil: Browning dish
Servings: 4

1 cup soft bread crumbs
1/3 cup milk
1 pound lean ground beef
1 egg slightly beaten
3 Tablespoons onion,
    chopped
1-1/2 teaspoons salt
1/4 teaspoon nutmeg
1/4 teaspoon allspice
pinch of pepper

1. In a mixing bowl, soak bread crumbs in milk 5 minutes. Add meat, egg, onions, salt, nutmeg, allspice and pepper. Mix together thoroughly. Shape into 16 meat balls or 32 miniature balls.

1-1/2 Tablespoons butter
1-1/2 Tablespoons flour
1/2 (10-¾ oz.) can beef
    broth
1/2 cup milk

2. Preheat browning dish 4½ minutes. Melt butter in dish and quickly brown meat balls. Cover with lid and microwave on **HIGH 3 MINUTES**. Turn meat balls over and continue to cook on **HIGH 3 MINUTES**. Remove meat balls from dish. Stir flour into butter. Add beef broth and milk slowly. Microwave on **HIGH 3 MINUTES**.

Put meat balls back in dish with gravy and cook on **HIGH 5 MINUTES**.

BRAISED BEEF RIBS/côtes de boeuf braisées

Cooking Time: 25 minutes plus browning time
Utensil: Browning dish
Servings: 4

4 pounds heavy beef ribs*
your favorite steak seasoning
and/or Liquid Smoke

1. Season ribs. Preheat browning dish **4 MINUTES ON HIGH** and brown ribs meaty side down. Wipe browning dish and preheat again to complete browning of all the meat.

2. Place meat back in dish meaty side up on a microsafe rack. Cover with lid or wax paper. Microwave on **MEDIUM 25 MINUTES.** Turn dish half way through cooking time.

*For better cooking results, have butcher cut ribs crosswise then between ribs.

SAVORY BEEF ROAST/rosbif succulent

Cooking Time: 6 to 8 minutes per pound
Utensil: Glass dish with a glass trivet
Servings: 6 to 10

**Rolled sirloin tip
(3 to 5 lbs.) or
Standing beef rib
roast (5 lbs.) (tie
with heavy string
around roast to keep
the shape)
Liquid Smoke seasoning
garlic powder
cracked black pepper**

1. Brush all sides of roast with Liquid Smoke. Rub with garlic powder (not garlic salt). Coat all surfaces with cracked black pepper, pressing pepper into roast.

2. Place roast cut side up on trivet in a glass dish. Cover roast with wax paper. Use Chart* to determine cooking time. Turn roast over half way through cooking time. Continue to cover. If meat thermometer is used, remove roast from Microwave when temperature reaches 10 to 15 degrees lower than the desired temperature. Let stand 10 to 15 minutes in foil tent—temperature will continue to increase.

CHART*

Roast Beef	Time Per Pound	Temp. After Standing Time
Rare	6½ minutes - **HIGH** (100%)	140
Medium	7½ minutes - **HIGH** (100%)	160
Well	8½ minutes - **HIGH** (100%)	170

CAJUN CHOP SUEY

Cooking Time: 25 minutes
Utensil: Browning skillet
Servings: 6

**2-1/2 lbs. pork, cut
into 1½" strips**

**2-1/2 cans (10-¾ oz. ea.)
bouillon
1/2 package dry onion soup
mix**

**2 bell peppers, shoestring
cut
1/2 package carrots, shoestring cut
1/2 bunch celery, shoe-
string cut
1 package frozen, French
cut green beans
1 bunch onion tops, cut
in 2½" lengths
2 Tablespoons flour**

1. Preheat browning skillet for 4½ minutes. Brown pork.

2. When meat is browned, add bouillon and onion soup. Cook on **HIGH 20 MINUTES** or until meat is tender. Cover.

3. Add all vegetables and flour. Cover with wax paper. Cook on **HIGH 5 MINUTES MORE,** or until vegetables are tender. Season to taste and add soy sauce if desired. Serve over hot rice.

Anita Guidry, "From Mama to Me."

CORN BEEF BRISKET

Serve along with Spinach Artichoke Soup.

Cooking Time: 35-40 minutes
Utensil: 3 quart casserole
Servings: 8-10 slices

**3-4 pound pre-seasoned
  corn beef brisket
2 cups hot water**

Bring hot water to boil in a 3 quart casserole. Add brisket, cover and cook on **HIGH 35-40 MINUTES.** Turn brisket over twice during cooking time. Remove from liquid, cover with plastic wrap and let stand 15 minutes. Liquid may be strained and used in Spinach Artichoke Soup on page 48.

COUNTRY TERRINE/terrine de campagne

Pistachios give the Terrine from Paris a flavorful taste.

Cooking Time: 18 minutes
Utensil: Terrine or ceramic loaf dish
Servings: 8-10

3/4 pound sliced bacon
1 Tablespoon butter
1 Tablespoon dehydrated
    onion
2 cloves garlic, crushed
1 pound lean pork,
    ground
1/2 pound veal, ground
1/2 pound chicken livers,
    finely chopped

1. Line the terrine (5" x 9" loaf dish) with bacon, reserving a few slices for the top. Melt butter in a 2 quart glass bowl. Add onion, garlic, pork, veal and chicken livers. Cover and cook on **HIGH 2 MINUTES.**

1/4 teaspoon allspice
pinch ground cloves
pinch ground nutmeg
2 eggs, beaten
1/2 cup cream
2 Tablespoons brandy
1-1/2 teaspoons salt
1/2 teaspoon pepper
1/2 cup shelled pistachios
1 slice cooked ham (1/2
    pound) cut in strips
1 bay leaf

2. Mix in allspice, cloves, nutmeg, eggs, cream, brandy, salt, pepper and pistachios. Stir until mixture holds together. Spread a 1/3 of the mixture in the lined dish, add a layer of 1/2 the ham slices and top with another 1/3 of the pork mixture. Add the remaining ham and cover with the last 1/3 of the pork. Lay the reserved bacon slices on top. Set the bay leaf on top of the bacon and add lid or wax paper. Cook on **HIGH 16 MINUTES,** turn dish 2 times.

The French keep the terrine in the refrigerator at least 3 days after cooking to allow the flavor to mellow before serving. It can be frozen for up to 3 months.

To serve, unmold the terrine, cut part of it in thick slices and arrange them overlapping on a platter. Serve cold or hot.

CREOLE CORN BREAD/pain de maïs créole

Goes good with red beans.

Cooking Time: 16 minutes
Utensils: Round glass dish
4-cup measuring cup
Servings: 6

1 Tablespoon olive oil
1 cup onion, chopped
1/2 pound lean ground meat
3 canned jalapeno peppers,
  seeded and chopped

1. In a 4-cup measure, sauté olive oil and onion on **HIGH 2 MINUTES**. Add meat, cover with wax paper. Cook on **HIGH 5 MINUTES**. Stir once during cooking time. Drain off fat. Add peppers.

1/2 cup yellow corn meal
1 egg, beaten
1/2 cup milk
3/4 teaspoon baking soda
1/2 teaspoon salt
1 (8½ oz.) can cream yellow
  corn
1/4 cup bacon fat

2. In a mixing bowl, combine corn meal, egg, milk, soda, salt, corn and bacon fat. Pour half of corn meal batter into a buttered round dish. *(Micro Memo: For more even cooking, place a small empty custard cup in center of dish).* Add all the meat mixture.

1-1/2 cups yellow cheese,
  grated
Crumbled bacon, optional

3. Spread cheese over meat and cover with rest of batter. Microwave on **HIGH 9 MINUTES**. Rotate dish every 3 minutes. Let stand 10 minutes before serving. Top may be sprinkled with bacon.

CREOLE JAMBALAYA/jambalaya créole

Jambalaya is a dish that is prepared from many different ingredients, but which always includes rice with whatever else is added.

Cooking Time: 46 minutes
Utensils: Browning skillet
          4 quart dish
Servings: 8

1 pound pork

1 Tablespoon butter,
      melted
1 cup onion, chopped
2 cloves garlic, minced

1. Cut pork in small squares. Preheat browning skillet on High 4 minutes. Brown or sear pork. Wipe out skillet, preheat on High 1½ minutes and repeat until all meat is browned. In a 4 quart dish, melt butter and sauté onion and garlic, covered, on **HIGH 6 MINUTES.**

12 small pork sausages,
      cut in bite size
1 slice ham, chopped
1/8 teaspoon thyme
2 bay leaves, minced
2 cloves, ground
2 Tablespoons parsley,
      chopped

2. Add pork, sausage, ham, thyme, bay leaves, cloves and parsley. Cover with wax paper and cook on **HIGH 5 MINUTES.**

1 quart beef broth
1/2 teaspoon chili peppers
1 teaspoon salt
1/2 teaspoon pepper
1/4 teaspoon cayenne pepper
1/2 teaspoon Chef Magic
1-1/2 cups uncooked rice
1/2 cup green onion tops,
      chopped

3. Add broth and seasonings. Cook covered on **HIGH 15 MINUTES,** stirring once or twice. Add rice and cover. Cook on **HIGH 20 MINUTES.** Add green onion and let stand covered 15 minutes.

GRILLADES & GRITS

Cooking Time: 42 minutes
Utensils: Browning dish
         4-cup measuring cup
Servings: 6-8

The round of the meat is always selected for Grillades (pronounced Gree-odds). The steak is cut into 6 or 8 squares and each piece is called "a grillade."

2 pounds beef or veal round, ½" thick

1. Cut meat into 6 or 8 individual servings. Preheat browning dish 4 minutes. Brown meat on both sides. It may be necessary to preheat the dish (1 minute 30 seconds) two more times to brown all the meat.

2 Tablespoons oil
2 Tablespoons flour
1 cup onion, sliced thin
1/2 cup green bell pepper, minced
1 Tablespoon parsley, chopped
3 cloves garlic, minced

2. Make a Roux with oil and flour in a 4-cup measure. Microwave on **HIGH 6 MINUTES,** stir two times. Add onion, green peppers, parsley and garlic. Microwave on **HIGH 6 MINUTES.** Stir at 3 minutes.

1 (14-½ oz.) can whole tomatoes, diced
1-1/2 teaspoons salt
1/4 teaspoon cayenne pepper
1/4 teaspoon pepper
1/2 teaspoon oregano

3. Stir in tomatoes, salt, pepper and oregano. Pour over meat in browning dish. Cover and microwave on **HIGH 30 MINUTES** or until meat is tender. Serve with grits. See page 161.

HAM LOAF

Flavor enhanced with Horseradish Sauce.

Cooking Time: 20 minutes
Utensil: 10" glass pie plate
Servings: 10

2 pounds lean pork,
   ground
1 cup cooked ham, ground
2 eggs, beaten
1/4 cup milk
1/4 cup oatmeal
1 cup cracker crumbs
1 Tablespoon Worcestershire
   sauce
1/2 teaspoon Spice Up (or
   your favorite)
1/4 teaspoon cayenne pepper
1/4 teaspoon garlic powder
2 Tablespoons chopped onions,
   dehydrated (or 1/4 cup
   fresh)

1. Microwave pork on **HIGH 4 MIN-
UTES** covered in a 10" pie plate
2" deep. Baste off any fat. Add
ham, eggs, milk, oatmeal, cracker
crumbs, Worcestershire sauce,
Spice Up, cayenne pepper, garlic
powder and onion. Mix together
thoroughly.

12 whole cloves
1 cup undiluted tomato
   soup

2. Stick cloves in meat and top with
tomato soup. Cover with wax
paper. Microwave on **HIGH 16
MINUTES.** Rotate dish 2 times.

HORSERADISH SAUCE
(optional)

3 Tablespoons horseradish
1/2 cup cream, whipped
1/2 teaspoon salt
squeeze of lemon juice

Mix horseradish, cream, salt and
lemon. Serve separately with Ham
Loaf.

HAM WITH MUSTARD GLAZE
jambon en gelée de moutarde

Cooking Time: 5 minutes per pound
Utensil: Microsafe cooking grill
in a 2 quart dish

Ham, precooked

1. Place ham fat side down on grill in a 2 quart dish. Cover loosely with wax paper. Cook on **MEDIUM 5 MINUTES PER POUND.** Turn ham over half way through cooking time and baste off accumulated liquid.

1/4 cup liquid brown sugar
1/2 teaspoon dry mustard
2 Tablespoons fruit juice

2. Combine sugar, mustard and juice. Baste ham with glaze during cooking. Standing time is 15-20 minutes.

Micro Memo:

If using a microwave safe thermometer, internal temperature must reach 130° during cooking. Leave thermometer in ham during standing time. Temperature should go to 150°.

LASAGNA/lasagne

Cooking Time: 33 minutes
Utensils: 2½ quart and 3 quart casseroles
Browning skillet
Servings: 8-10

1/2 pound lasagna noodles
4 cups water
1 teaspoon olive oil
1 teaspoon salt

1. In a 2½ quart casserole, add salt and oil to water and bring to boil on High. Place pasta in casserole. Microwave on **HIGH 10 MINUTES**, covered. Drain. (If time is short, cook pasta conventionally while preparing sauce in the microwave).

1 pound ground round
1 clove garlic, minced

2. Preheat browning skillet 4 minutes. Brown meat, add garlic, cover and microwave on **HIGH 3 MINUTES**.

1 envelope dry onion
soup mix
1-1/4 cups water
1 (6 oz.) can tomato paste
1 (8 oz.) can tomato sauce
1 teaspoon salt
1/2 teaspoon pepper
1 teaspoon oregano

3. Blend in onion soup, water, tomato paste, tomato sauce, salt, pepper and oregano. Stir well. Cover and microwave on **HIGH 10 MINUTES**, stirring every 3 minutes.

1/2 pound mozzarella cheese,
sliced or grated
1 pound cottage cheese
Parmesan cheese

4. Layer meat mixture, noodles, mozzarella cheese and cottage cheese in a flat 3 quart casserole. Repeat layers, ending with meat sauce. Sprinkle top with Parmesan cheese. Microwave on **HIGH 10 MINUTES** or until heated through. Rotate dish 2 times.

MEAT LOAF I/pain de viande en barbecue

When you are in a hurry.

Cooking Time: 15 minutes
Utensil: 10″ glass pie plate
Servings: 6

2 pounds lean ground beef
1 large package Lawry's
    meat loaf seasoning
1-1/2 cups water

Mix meat, seasoning and water together. Place in a 10″ glass pie plate. Cover loosely with wax paper. Cook on **HIGH 7 MINUTES**. Baste off accumulated fat. Turn dish. Continue cooking covered on **HIGH 7 MORE MINUTES**.

MEAT LOAF TOPPING

1/3 cup catsup
2 teaspoons Worcestershire
    Sauce

Combine catsup and Worcestershire Sauce. Spread on meat loaf. Reheat meat loaf 1 minute.

MEAT LOAF II

Cooking Time: 17 minutes
Utensil: 2 quart casserole
Servings: 8

2 pounds ground round
    steak
2 eggs, beaten
1/2 cup catsup
1-1/2 cups bread crumbs
1 package onion soup mix
1/2 cup warm water
1 teaspoon Accent

Combine meat, eggs, catsup, bread crumbs, soup mix, water and Accent in a 2 quart casserole. Mix together thoroughly. Level mixture, cover with wax paper and cook on **HIGH 17 MINUTES**. Rotate the dish and baste off accumulated fat two times. Let stand 5 minutes.

MILLARD'S BEEF CASSEROLE
boeuf casserole de Millard

Cooking Time: 30 minutes
Utensil: 3 quart casserole
Servings: 4

**2 pounds beef, cubed
(sirloin tip)
3-4 carrots, sliced thin
2 cups onion, sliced**

1. Place beef, carrots and onions in a 3 quart casserole.

**1/4 cup flour
1/2 cup bread crumbs
1 Tablespoon parsley
flakes**

2. Mix flour, bread crumbs and parsley together. Sprinkle over meat.

**1-1/2 teaspoons salt
1/2 teaspoon ground black
pepper
3/4 cup red wine
3/4 cup beef consomme
undiluted**

3. Stir salt and pepper into wine and consomme. Pour over ingredients in the casserole. Cover. Microwave on **HIGH 15 MINUTES.** Stir and continue cooking on **HIGH 15 MINUTES** covered.

BREADED PORK CHOPS/côtes de porc panées

Cooking Time: 32 minutes
Utensil: 2 quart pyrex baking dish
Servings: 6

1 clove garlic, chopped
    fine
1/2 cup butter

1 Tablespoon parsley,
    chopped fine
1 teaspoon salt
1/2 teaspoon cayenne pepper
1/4 teaspoon onion powder
1/4 teaspoon black pepper
1 cup dry bread crumbs
6 pork chops (6-8 oz. each)

1. In a 2 quart baking dish, sauté garlic in butter on **HIGH 2 MINUTES.**

2. Combine parsley, salt, cayenne pepper, onion powder, black pepper and bread crumbs together in a flat dish. Dip chops in garlic butter, then roll in seasoned bread crumbs. Place in baking dish. Sprinkle remaining bread crumbs over chops. Cover with wax paper and microwave on **HIGH 15 MINUTES,** turn chops over and microwave **15 MINUTES** or until well done.

PORK CHOP CASSEROLE

Cooking Time: 31 minutes
Utensils: Browning skillet
4-cup glass measuring cup
Servings: 4-6

4 to 6 pork chops (2-3 lbs.)
salt
pepper

1. Preheat browning skillet on High 4 minutes. Place 2 or 3 pork chops at a time in skillet, quickly turn to sear other side. Cover with lid or wax paper and cook on **HIGH 3 MINUTES.** Wipe out skillet and preheat again for 4 minutes and repeat procedure. After browning, season meat with salt and pepper.

1/2 cup uncooked rice
1 (10-¾ oz.) can undiluted beef consomme
1 teaspoon Worcestershire sauce
1/2 teaspoon garlic salt

2. Place rice, consomme, Worcestershire sauce and garlic salt in a 4-cup measure. Cover and microwave on **HIGH 5 MINUTES.** Remove meat from browning dish. Pour in hot rice mixture and place pork chops on top of rice. Cover and cook on **HIGH 20 MINUTES** or until rice and meat are cooked.

SPAGHETTI & MEAT SAUCE/spaghetti bolognaise

Cooking Time: 35 minutes
Utensil: 3 quart casserole
Makes 2 quarts

2 pounds lean ground meat
1 cup onion, chopped
1/2 cup celery, finely
    chopped
3 cloves garlic, minced

1. In a 3 quart casserole, mix together meat, onion, celery and garlic. Cover. Cook on **HIGH 10 MINUTES**, stirring twice. Drain off fat.

1 (28 oz.) can tomatoes,
    chopped
1 (12 oz.) can tomato paste
2 teaspoons salt
1/2 teaspoon pepper
1 Tablespoon Worcestershire
    Sauce
1 Tablespoon dry parsley
    flakes
1 teaspoon basil
1/2 teaspoon oregano
1 bay leaf

2. Stir in tomatoes and liquid, tomato paste, salt, pepper, Worcestershire Sauce, parsley, basil, oregano and bay leaf. Cover. Cook on **HIGH 25 MINUTES**, stirring twice. Remove bay leaf.

Cooked spaghetti (3 cups
    will serve 4-5)
Parmesan cheese

3. Serve sauce over spaghetti. Sprinkle with Parmesan cheese. Freeze remaining sauce.

NOT JUST PLAIN STEW/ragoût de boeuf

Cooking Time: 50 minutes
Utensil: Browning dish
Servings: 4-6

**2 pounds stew meat
  (cut up)
1 (10-¾ oz.) can mushroom
  soup, undiluted
1 (10-¾ oz.) can onion
  soup, undiluted**

1. Preheat browning dish for 4½ minutes. Brown meat for 1 minute on both sides. Stir mushroom and onion soup into meat in browning dish. Cover and cook on **MEDIUM 50 MINUTES.**

2. Allow 10 minutes standing time.

Dressing/Rice

Eggs/Sauce

Dressings:

Dressings can be served all year long as casseroles or used during the holiday season as stuffing for turkey.

Rice:

You won't find many meals in Louisiana served without rice, everyone enjoys it. Rice is the main ingredient in many of the **Tout de Suite** recipes and is always served with gumbo, stew, and of course, étouffée!

Eggs:

Eggs cook more evenly in the Microwave when the egg yolks and whites are mixed for omelets and quiche. Both are a delightful change for a luncheon or dinner.

Sauce:

A plain, simple meal becomes a gourmet's delight with an elegant sauce enhancing fish, fowl, meat and eggs.

BEEF BROTH RICE DRESSING/farce pot-au-feu

Cooking Time: 22 minutes
Utensil: 2 quart dish
Servings: 4

3 Tablespoons butter, melted
1/2 cup green bell pepper, minced
3/4 cup green onion tops, minced

1. In a 2 quart dish, sauté butter, green pepper and onion tops on **HIGH 3 MINUTES.**

2 cups canned beef or chicken broth
1/4 teaspoon pepper
1/4 cup parsley, minced

2. Stir in broth, pepper and parsley — mix well. Cover and bring to boil on **HIGH 5 MINUTES.**

1 cup raw white rice

3. Stir in rice and cover with wax paper. Microwave on **HIGH 14 MINUTES**—or until rice is tender.

RICE AND OYSTER DRESSING
farce au riz et aux huîtres

Cooking Time: 17 minutes
Utensils: Browning dish
             3 quart casserole
Servings: 6-8

1 pound chicken livers
1 Tablespoon butter

1. Preheat browning dish 4 minutes. Sauté chicken livers in butter. Cook on **HIGH 2 MINUTES.** Cut in small pieces and set aside.

1/2 cup butter
10 green onions, chopped
1 cup celery, chopped
1/2 cup green peppers,
**   chopped**

2. In a 3 quart casserole, micromelt butter on **HIGH 1 MINUTE.** Stir in onions, celery and green peppers. Cover with wax paper. Sauté on **HIGH 4 MINUTES** or until tender.

1 quart raw oysters, drained
**   or 4 (8 oz.) cans oysters**
1/2 cup parsley, chopped
3 cups cooked rice
1 teaspoon salt
1/2 teaspoon cayenne pepper
1/4 teaspoon black pepper
1/2 teaspoon Tabasco

3. Add oysters, livers, parsley, rice, salt, pepper and Tabasco. Cover. Cook on **HIGH 10 MINUTES.**

CORN BREAD DRESSING/farce au pain de maïs

Stuff the turkey or place in a casserole dish.

Cooking Time: 55-58 minutes
Utensils: 4 quart casserole dish
Browning skillet
Makes 3 quarts

1-1/2 pounds ground pork
1/2 cup butter
3 cloves garlic, minced
3/4 cup celery, minced
3/4 cup bell pepper,
chopped
1-1/2 cups onion, chopped

1. Preheat browning skillet 4 minutes. Brown pork and sauté covered on **HIGH 15 MINUTES,** stirring every 3 minutes. Pour off any accumulated fat. Add butter, garlic, celery, bell pepper and onion. Sauté covered on **HIGH 15-18 MINUTES,** stirring every 6 minutes until vegetables are tender. Transfer to a 4 quart dish.

2 beef bouillon cubes
2 cups water
1 Tablespoon Kitchen
Bouquet
1 teaspoon salt
1/2 teaspoon cayenne pepper
1 teaspoon allspice
1/2 cup parsley, chopped
1/2 cup green onions,
chopped
corn bread (opposite page)

2. Add bouillon, water and seasonings. Cover and cook on **HIGH 15 MINUTES.** Set aside until ready to mix with corn bread (see recipe on page 137).

3. Crumble corn bread and add to meat mixture. Stop adding when dressing is at right moisture level. If too dry, add more bouillon. Stuff turkey, chicken, or place in a casserole dish. Cover with wax paper or plastic wrap and microwave on **HIGH 5 MINUTES** or until heated through.

CORN BREAD FOR STUFFING

Cooking Time: 5 minutes
Utensil: Browning skillet

1 cup yellow corn meal
1 cup all-purpose flour,
   sifted
4 teaspoons baking powder
1/2 teaspoon salt

1. Sift together corn meal, flour, baking powder and salt.

1 egg, beaten
1 cup evaporated milk
1/4 cup cooking oil

2. Blend in egg, milk and oil. Beat until smooth. Spray browning skillet with vegetable oil, preheat 2 minutes. Pour in batter and cook on **HIGH 3 MINUTES.** Turn dish and cook on **HIGH 2 MINUTES.** Let stand 10 minutes and turn out on plate.

EGGPLANT AND RICE CASSEROLE
riz et aubergine casserole

With meat or shrimp!

Cooking Time: 30 minutes
Utensils: 2 quart dish
          3 quart casserole
Servings: 6-8

2 medium eggplants, peeled
  and diced
2 Tablespoons water
1/2 teaspoon salt

1. Place eggplant and water mixed with salt in a 2 quart dish. Cover with plastic wrap. Cook on **HIGH 7 MINUTES.** Stir and drain. Set aside.

1/2 cup butter, melted
2 cups onion, chopped
1/2 cup celery, chopped

2. Melt butter in a 3 quart casserole. Sauté onion and celery on **HIGH 5 MINUTES.**

1/2 cup green onions,
  chopped
1/4 cup parsley, chopped
4 cloves garlic, minced

3. Add green onions, parsley and garlic. Sauté on **HIGH 3 MINUTES.**

1/2 pound lean ground meat
  or
1 pound raw peeled shrimp
2 cups cooked rice
2 teaspoons salt
1/2 teaspoon black pepper
1/2 teaspoon cayenne pepper
seasoned bread crumbs
Parmesan cheese

4. Stir in ground meat or shrimp, mix well. Cover with wax paper and microwave on **HIGH 10 MINUTES.** Stir two times. Drain off fat. Add rice, eggplant, salt and pepper. Stir to mix. Top with seasoned bread crumbs and Parmesan cheese. Cover. Microwave on **MEDIUM 5 MINUTES** or until heated through.

138

MICROWAVE RICE/riz en hyperfréquence

Cooking Time: 10-12 minutes
Utensil: 2½ quart casserole
Servings: 4

2 cups hot water
1 cup long grain rice,
    uncooked
1/2 teaspoon salt

Place water in a 2½ quart casserole. Microwave until boiling (approximately 5 minutes on high). Add rice and salt. Cover with wax paper and cook on **HIGH 5 MINUTES.** Stir, cover and cook another **5-7 MINUTES ON HIGH.** Stir and let stand, covered, several minutes before serving.

RICE PILAF/riz pilaf

A flavorful dish from Paris.

Cooking Time: 28 minutes
Utensil: 2 quart dish
Makes 4 cups

3 Tablespoons butter
1 cup onion, finely
  chopped
1-1/2 cups uncooked rice

3 cups hot chicken stock
  (in which white wine
  was added)
Bouquet garni (1 parsley
  stem, 1 bay leaf and
  thyme wrapped in a
  green onion stem)
1 teaspoon salt
1/4 teaspoon white pepper

1. In a 2 quart dish, sauté 2 Table-spoons butter and onion on **HIGH 6 MINUTES.** Stir one time. Add rice, cover with wax paper and cook on **HIGH 2 MINUTES.**

2. Add stock, the bouquet garni, salt and pepper. Cover with plastic wrap and cook on **HIGH 20 MIN-UTES.** Stir half way through cooking time. Let stand covered 10 minutes. Remove bouquet garni. Dot top with remaining butter, stir with a fork to fluff rice, and taste for seasoning.

SHRIMP JAMBALAYA/jambalaya aux crevettes

A Spanish-Creole dish pronounced Jum-ba-lí-a

Cooking Time: 19 minutes
Utensils: 4-cup glass measuring cup
        3 quart casserole
Servings: 6

3 Tablespoons oil
3 Tablespoons flour

1. Mix oil and flour together in a 4-cup measure. Cook on **HIGH 5-6 MINUTES** until Roux is a light brown (not dark as for gumbo and stew). Stir.

2 cups onion, chopped
    fine
1/2 cup green bell pepper,
    chopped fine
4 garlic cloves, chopped fine

2. Add onions, green pepper and garlic. Sauté on **HIGH 3 MINUTES**. Pour into a 3 quart casserole.

1 (10 oz.) can Ro-tel
    tomatoes, chopped
1-1/2 cups hot water
2 cups raw shrimp, peeled

3. Stir in tomatoes and liquid, water and shrimp. Cover. Cook on **HIGH 7 MINUTES** until shrimp are pink.

2 teaspoons salt
2 cups diced ham
3 cups cooked rice
1 Tablespoon parsley, chopped
1 Tablespoon green onion
    tops, chopped

4. Add ham, salt and cooked rice. Mix well. Cover. Cook on **HIGH 3 MINUTES**. Garnish with parsley and onion tops.

The Creole name jambalaya is derived from the French word for ham (jambon). This is just one of many different ingredients that can go into the pot. Seafood, vegetables, meats are acceptable jambalaya ingredients, but most important is rice which is always included.

BACON 'N' EGGS

Cooking Time: Bacon — 6-8 minutes
                     Eggs — 2-3 minutes
Utensils: plate
                browning skillet
Servings: 4

BACON

3 Methods:

(1) Place 8 slices of bacon between layers of paper towels on a dinner plate or paper plate. Microwave on **HIGH 6-8 MINUTES.** Timing depends on temperature and thickness of slices. A fairly good timing is 1 minute per slice. Bacon is always uniformly crisp and clean-up is quick.

(2) When saving bacon fat for other recipes, microwave bacon on a dinner plate covered with wax paper. Pour off fat once during cooking time.

(3) The third method is a microwave safe Bacon Rack with a well to collect fat. Cover with wax paper or a paper towel. Timing should be the same for all 3 methods if fat is removed in (2) and (3). Bacon will stay warm covered with a paper towel while eggs are cooking.

EGGS

Preheat browning skillet on High 3 minutes. Place a pat of butter in each corner and as it melts, quickly put in 4 eggs. (It is not necessary to pierce the yolks if you cover with lid, but if you use wax paper, it will be necessary). Microwave covered on **HIGH 2 MINUTES.** For a firmer yolk, check eggs at 2 minutes and add 30 seconds to 1 minute more. Eggs will continue to cook slightly, but will stay warm if left to sit covered in the browning skillet.

EGGS HUSSARDE/oeufs hussarde

Cooking Time: Approximately 22 minutes
Utensil: Plate
Servings: 6

3/4 cup marchand de vin sauce

1. Prepare marchand de vin sauce on page 152. (Freeze sauce not used).

2/3 cup Hollandaise sauce

2. Prepare Hollandaise Sauce on page 151.

6 slices ham, warmed
6 soft poached eggs
3 English muffins, split
paprika

3. Place ham on a plate, cover with wax paper and cook on **HIGH 2 MINUTES.**

4. Poach eggs and toast muffins conventionally or in the microwave.

To assemble eggs hussarde, place a slice of ham across a split English muffin and cover with marchand de vin sauce. Place a poached egg on sauce and top with Hollandaise sauce. Garnish with a sprinkling of paprika.

EGGS JOLENE/oeufs jolene

Breakfast or brunch for two.

Cooking Time: 1 minute per egg
Utensil: 2 ramekins
Servings: 2

**2 slices of bread,
   crumbled**

1. Line 2 ramekins with soft bread. Cover each with 2 Tablespoons of one of the following minced fillings: cooked chicken, sausage or ham; or sautéed mushrooms.

**2 eggs
2 Tablespoons cream
salt and pepper
buttered bread crumbs
optional:
   1 Tablespoon parsley
   pimento**

2. Slip an egg into each ramekin. Top with 1 Tablespoon cream, salt, pepper and bread crumbs. Puncture yolk with wooden pick, cover with wax paper and cook on **HIGH 1 MINUTE** per egg. For a firmer egg, cook 30 seconds per egg longer. Garnish with parsley and pimento.

EGGS IN A RAMEKIN

Cooking Time: 10 minutes
Utensils: 1 quart dish
            2 ramekins
Servings: 2

**10 oz. package frozen,
    chopped spinach
1 teaspoon beef bouillon
    granules**

**2 eggs
salt and pepper
2 Tablespoons cream
1/2 cup yellow cheese,
    grated**

1. Cook spinach and bouillon covered in a 1 quart dish on **HIGH 7 MINUTES.** Drain. Line bottom of 2 ramekins with spinach.

2. Slip an egg into each ramekin. Sprinkle with salt and pepper. Pour 1 Tablespoon of cream over each egg. Sprinkle grated cheese on top.

3. Puncture yolk with a wooden pick. Place 2 ramekins in the Microwave. Cover with wax paper. Cook on **HIGH 3 MINUTES** or until eggs are softly cooked.

EGG WHITE OMELET

Cooking Time: 8½ minutes
Utensils: 2-cup glass measuring cup
9" glass pie plate
Servings: 2 or 3

FILLING

1 Tablespoon butter
2 Tablespoons onion, chopped
2 Tablespoons bell pepper, chopped
1/2 cup sliced mushrooms
2 teaspoons soy sauce

1. Melt butter in a 2-cup measure on **HIGH 30 SECONDS.** Sauté onion and bell pepper on **HIGH 2 MINUTES.** Add mushrooms and soy sauce. Cook on **HIGH 1 MINUTE.** Set aside.

OMELET

1 Tablespoon butter
6 egg whites
2 teaspoons powdered skim milk
4 drops yellow food coloring

2. Melt butter in a 9" glass pie plate. Beat egg whites, powdered milk and food coloring until stiff. Pour into buttered pie plate and microwave on **HIGH 5 MINUTES.** Rotate dish several times so omelet will cook evenly. Place filling on half of the omelet. Slip long spatula under unfilled side—lift and flip over to cover filling. Cut omelet in 2 or 3 wedges.

ELEGANT OMELET/omelette élégante

Fill it your way!

Cooking Time: 5 minutes
Utensil: 9" pie plate
Servings: 3-4

Prepare 1½ to 2 cups of omelet filling.*

1 Tablespoon butter
4 eggs, separated
1/4 cup milk
1/2 teaspoon salt
dash pepper

1. Melt butter in a 9" pie plate. Mix together yolks, milk, salt and pepper. Beat egg whites until stiff. Fold yolks into whites with a spatula. Pour into pie plate leveling mixture. Cook on **HIGH 5 MINUTES,** turn dish once.

OMELET FILLINGS*

chopped ham and cheese
cooked shrimp, crawfish
    or crabmeat
chopped artichoke hearts
crumbled bacon
cheddar cheese, grated
oysters sautéed with
    shallots
picante sauce
sautéed chicken livers
sautéed mushrooms
sautéed okra

2. Place filling of your choice on half of the omelet. Slip long spatula under unfilled side—lift and flip over to cover filling. Cut omelet in 3 or 4 wedges.

LOST BREAD/pain perdu

PAIN PERDU in French literally means "lost bread" which refers to the fact that stale bread might be lost if not made into this delightful breakfast toast, also called French Toast. Bread is dipped into a seasoned egg mixture, then cooked until brown on each side and sprinkled with confectioners sugar before serving.

Cooking Time: 6 minutes
Utensil: Browning skillet
Servings: 3-4

3 large eggs
3/4 cup sugar
1 cup evaporated milk
1 Tablespoon vanilla
1/2 teaspoon cinnamon
10-12 slices white bread,
   stale (French bread is
   preferred)

1. In a 10" glass pie plate, whisk eggs. Beat in sugar and add milk, vanilla and cinnamon. Dip bread slices in mixture until soaked.

3 Tablespoons butter,
   melted

2. Preheat browning skillet on High 4 minutes. Pour 1 Tablespoon of butter in skillet, quickly put in 4 slices of soaked bread. Turn immediately to brown both sides. Cover with wax paper and microwave on HIGH 1 MINUTE. Turn slices over, cook on HIGH 1 MINUTE. Repeat process for next 4 slices. Serve plain or with powdered sugar or syrup.

Micro Memo:

Pain Perdu can be made ahead and wrapped individually in plastic wrap. Heat in wrap on HIGH 1 MINUTE per slice.

CAJUN QUICHE/Quiche Cajun

With crab and crawfish.

Cooking Time: 14 minutes
Utensil: 10" quiche or
glass pie plate
Servings: 6

10" cooked pastry shell
1 cup Swiss cheese,
shredded
1/2 pound crabmeat,
drained
1/2 pound peeled crawfish
or shrimp, cooked
2 green onions, finely
chopped

1. Recipe for pastry on page 195. Cool shell. Sprinkle cheese evenly over bottom of pie shell. Top with crabmeat and crawfish or shrimp, then green onion.

4 eggs, beaten
1 cup whipping cream
1/2 teaspoon salt
1/8 teaspoon cayenne pepper

2. Mix beaten eggs, cream, salt and pepper. Pour over mixture in pie shell. Microwave on **HIGH 9 MINUTES.** Stir gently once or twice during cooking time. Center will still wiggle, but will finish cooking while standing a few minutes.

QUICHE LORRAINE

Cooking Time: 22 minutes
Utensil: 9" glass pie plate
Servings: 6

**9" baked pastry shell
(If frozen, remove from
foil pan to glass pie
plate)**

Recipe for pastry on pages 194 & 195.

1. Cool pie shell.

**8 slices bacon, cooked
and crumbled
1-1/2 cups Swiss cheese,
shredded
1/4 cup onion, minced**

2. Cook bacon covered approximately 1 minute per slice. Crumble. Sprinkle bacon, cheese and onion in cooled pie shell.

**4 eggs
1 (13 oz.) can evaporated
milk
1/2 teaspoon salt
1/4 teaspoon cayenne pepper**

3. Beat eggs, milk, salt and pepper with a wire wisk until well blended. Pour over cheese mixture in pastry. Microwave on **HIGH 8-9 MINUTES.** Stir gently and turn dish once or twice during cooking time. Center will still wiggle, but will finish cooking while standing for a few minutes.

HOLLANDAISE SAUCE

Cooking Time: 2 minutes
Utensil: 2-cup glass measuring cup
Makes 2/3 cup

1/4 cup butter
1 Tablespoon lemon juice
2 egg yolks, beaten
2 Tablespoons light cream
1/2 teaspoon dry mustard
1/4 teaspoon salt
dash Tabasco

Place butter in a 2-cup glass measure. Microwave on **HIGH 1 MIN-UTE.** Stir in lemon juice, egg yolks, cream, mustard, salt and Tabasco. Microwave on **HIGH 1 MINUTE,** stirring every 15 seconds. Beat with a wire wisk until smooth. Sauce can be reheated on High 1 minute.

MARCHAND DE VIN SAUCE

Cooking Time: 19 minutes
Utensil: 4-cup glass measuring cup
Makes 3½ cups

1/2 cup butter, melted
1/3 cup green onion tops,
    finely chopped
1/2 cup onion, finely
    chopped
4 cloves garlic, minced

1. Melt butter in a 4-cup measuring cup. Sauté green onion, onion and garlic on **HIGH 5 MINUTES.**

3/4 cup cooked ham,
    minced
1/2 cup mushrooms, finely
    chopped, fresh or canned
2 Tablespoons flour
1/2 teaspoon salt
1/8 teaspoon pepper
1/8 teaspoon cayenne pepper

2. Add ham and mushrooms. Cook on **HIGH 2 MINUTES.** Stir in flour, salt and pepper. Cover with wax paper and cook on **HIGH 2 MINUTES.**

1 cup beef stock (can be
    made with 1-1/2 tea-
    spoons of Beef Flavor
    Base and 1 cup hot
    water)
1/2 cup red wine

3. Stir in beef stock and red wine. Cover with wax paper. Cook on **HIGH 10 MINUTES.** Stir once. Sauce can be frozen.

MUSHROOM SAUCE/sauce aux champignons
FOR MEAT OR POULTRY

Cooking Time: 14 minutes
Utensil: 2 quart glass dish
Servings: 6

1/2 cup butter

1. Micromelt butter in a 2 quart glass dish on **HIGH 1 MINUTE.**

2 cups onion, diced
1 beef or chicken
    bouillon cube
1 teaspoon garlic powder
1 teaspoon seasoned
    pepper

2. Sauté onion, bouillon cube, garlic powder and pepper in butter and cook on **HIGH 8 MINUTES.** Stir after one half of cooking time.

2 Tablespoons flour
1/4 cup water
1 pound fresh mushrooms,
    rinsed and dried
1/4 cup red wine

3. Stir in flour, add water slowly. Add mushrooms and wine. Cover. Cook on **HIGH 5 MINUTES.** Sauce can be frozen and reheated.

Vegetables

Vegetables:
    The beautiful natural color of both fresh and frozen vegetables is retained when cooked with little or no water in the Microwave.

ASPARAGUS AU GRATIN/asperges au gratin

Cooking Time: 6 minutes
Utensils: 4-cup glass measuring cup
         3 quart casserole
Servings: 6

1/4 cup butter
1 (10 oz.) can mushroom
   soup, concentrated
2 hard boiled eggs,
   chopped

3/4 cup cracker crumbs
1 (14 oz.) can asparagus
   spears, drained
3/4 cup mild cheddar cheese,
   grated

1. Heat soup and butter in a 4-cup measure on **HIGH 2 MINUTES.** Stir in chopped eggs.

2. In a 3 quart casserole, layer crumbs, asparagus, soup and egg mixture then grated cheese. Repeat layers and top with crumbs.

3. Cook on **HIGH 4 MINUTES** or until heated through.

PICKLED BEETS/betteraves marinées

Cooking Time: 7 minutes
Utensil: 1½ or 2 quart covered casserole
Servings: 4

1/4 cup onion, chopped
1 Tablespoon cooking oil

1. Sauté onion and cooking oil in a 2 quart casserole for **3 MINUTES ON HIGH.** Stir once.

1 teaspoon sugar
2 Tablespoons vinegar
1/4 teaspoon black pepper
1/4 teaspoon salt
1/4 cup bell pepper,
    chopped
1 (16 oz.) can beets, drained
    and sliced

2. Add sugar, vinegar, pepper, salt, bell pepper and beets. Cover. Microwave on **HIGH 4 MINUTES.** Stir once.

May be served hot or cold.

BROCCOLI CASSEROLE

Cooking Time: 18 minutes
Utensils: 1½ quart dish
    2 quart casserole
Servings: 6

3 Tablespoons oil
1/2 cup onion, chopped

1. Sauté onion in oil in a 1½ quart dish on **HIGH 3 MINUTES.**

2 (10 oz.) packages frozen chopped broccoli

2. Add broccoli, cover with wax paper, and continue cooking **7 MINUTES ON HIGH.** Stir once or twice.

6 slices American cheese
1 (10-¾ oz.) can cream of mushroom soup, undiluted

3. Spoon half the broccoli mixture into a 2 quart casserole. Layer with ½ the cheese and ½ of the undiluted soup.

1-1/2 cups bread crumbs
1/2 cup butter

4. Combine bread crumbs with butter until well coated and layer ½ the crumbs over soup. Repeat layers topping with bread crumbs. Cover with wax paper. Microwave on **HIGH 8 MINUTES.** Turn dish two times during cooking time.

BROCCOLI & HERBS/brocoli aux fines herbs

Easy and tasty.

Cooking Time: 16 minutes
Utensils: 2 quart casserole
          2-cup glass measuring cup
Servings: 6

2 (10 oz.) packages frozen broccoli spears

1. Cook broccoli in packages (puncture box) on **HIGH 7 MINUTES** each. Drain and place in a 2 quart casserole.

1/4 cup butter, melted
4 Tablespoons lemon juice
1/4 teaspoon garlic powder
1/4 teaspoon salt
1/4 teaspoon ground black pepper
1/4 teaspoon oregano
1/4 teaspoon sweet basil
1/4 teaspoon tarragon

2. Melt butter in a 2-cup measure. Add lemon juice, garlic, salt, pepper, oregano, basil and tarragon. Microwave on **HIGH 1½-2 MINUTES**. Pour over broccoli.

CORN ON THE COB/maïs sur l'épi

Three methods — try them all.

Corn can be 1) cooked directly in husks or 2) wrapped in wax paper, plastic wrap or 3) placed in a large plastic bag. After cooking for all methods, wrap corn in a dish towel and let stand 3 to 5 minutes. Corn will stay warm 15 minutes if kept wrapped or put into a grocery bag until serving time. Arrange corn ears in a triangle or square in the microwave. Rotate and rearrange half way through cooking time.

Method 1) Corn should be completely enclosed in husk. Secure ends with rubber bands. After 3-5 minutes standing time, husks can be pulled back, silks removed and husks put back in place. If serving outdoors, twist husks to make a convenient handle.

Method 2) Remove husk and silk and wrap each ear individually in plastic wrap or wax paper.

Method 3) 4 ears of corn can be placed in a plastic bag after removing husk and silk. Corn can be easily buttered and salted before cooking.

APPROXIMATE COOKING TIME

1 ear — 2 minutes
2 ears — 4 to 6 minutes
3 ears — 6 to 8 minutes

4 ears — 8 to 10 minutes
6 ears — 9 to 11 minutes

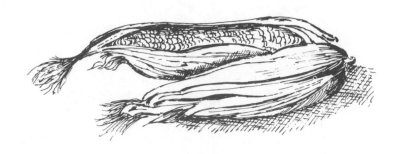

CHEESE GRITS/semoule de maïs au four

Cooking Time: 11 minutes
Utensil: 2 quart glass casserole
Servings: 6-8

1/2 cup grits
2 cups water

1. Bring water to boil in a 2 quart casserole. Add grits, cover with wax paper and microwave on **HIGH 3 MINUTES.**

1/3 cup butter
2 eggs, well beaten
1 (6 oz.) roll Kraft's garlic
    cheese, chopped

2. Add butter and stir in eggs slowly. Add chopped up cheese and stir until melted. Microwave covered on **MEDIUM 8 MINUTES,** turning 2 or 3 times. Let stand 5 minutes before serving.

GRITS

Cooking Time: 5 minutes
Utensil: 8-cup glass measuring cup
Servings: 4

1/2 cup quick grits
2 cups water
1/2 teaspoon salt

1. In an 8-cup measuring cup, mix grits, water and salt.

2 Tablespoons butter

2. Cover with wax paper. Cook **5 MINUTES ON HIGH.** Add butter.

Leftover tip: Refrigerate grits. When firm, cut in squares, cover with wax paper, and reheat on **HIGH 2 MINUTES.**

GREEN BEAN CASSEROLE
haricots verts casserole

Cooking Time: 24 minutes
Utensils: 2 quart casserole
         4-cup glass measuring cup
Servings: 4

4 strips of bacon (instructions on page 142)

1. Microwave bacon until crisp. Remove bacon from fat, crumble and set aside.

1/2 cup onion, chopped
1 cup celery, chopped
1/4 cup bell pepper, chopped
2 Tablespoons bacon fat

2. Sauté onion, celery and bell pepper in 2 Tablespoons of bacon fat on **HIGH 4 MINUTES** in a 4-cup measure.

1 (16 oz.) can whole tomatoes, cut up and drained
1/4 teaspoon salt
1/8 teaspoon pepper
1/2 pound American cheese, grated

3. Add tomatoes, salt and pepper. Cook on **HIGH 5 MINUTES**. Stir in cheese.

2 (16 oz.) cans green beans, drained

4. Place drained beans in casserole dish. Top with sauce and crumbled bacon. Cover with wax paper and microwave on **MEDIUM 15 MINUTES**. Rotate dish once during cooking time.

MAQUECHOU

Maquechou (pronounced mock shoe) is Indian-style stewed corn and tomatoes.

Cooking Time: 23 minutes
Utensil: 3 quart casserole
Servings: 6

10 ears fresh corn
or
2 (16 oz.) cans whole corn,
drained or
4 cups frozen corn kernels,
defrosted

1. For fresh corn: Cut top part of kernels from cob with sharp knife. Use back of knife and rub over cob to press out milk. For canned corn: Use electric can opener!

1/4 cup butter or bacon fat
1-1/2 cups onion, chopped
1/2 cup green bell pepper,
chopped
1 clove garlic, minced

2. Micromelt fat in a 3 quart dish. Sauté onion, bell pepper and garlic on **HIGH 3 MINUTES** or until tender.

1 (10 oz.) can Ro-tel
tomatoes, chopped,
with liquid
1 teaspoon salt

3. Add corn, tomatoes and salt. Cover with wax paper. Cook on **HIGH 20 MINUTES**. Stir once or twice. Cooking time will be shorter for canned corn.

Variation: For **SEAFOOD MAQUECHOU** add 1 pound cooked shrimp or crawfish during the last 5 minutes of cooking.

MIRLITONS WITH SHRIMP/mirliton aux crevettes

MIRLITON (pronounced by many as melly-ton) is the Haitian-French name for the vegetable pear. It grows on a vine and is from the cucumber and squash family. Mirlitons are prepared like eggplant or squash.

Cooking Time: 34 minutes
Utensils: 2 quart glass dish
            Flat plate
Servings: 6

3 mirlitons
3 slices bread, torn in
    small pieces

3 Tablespoons bacon fat
    or butter
1/2 cup onion, minced
3 cloves garlic, minced
1/4 cup green onion tops,
    chopped
1/4 cup celery, chopped
1 egg, slightly beaten
2 teaspoons salt
1/2 teaspoon pepper
1/2 teaspoon cayenne pepper
1 cup cooked shrimp, cut
    in bite size pieces
1 Tablespoon parsley
Bread crumbs

1. Slice mirlitons in halves lengthwise (remove seed) and place in a plastic bag. Close end of bag with a rubber band and place bagged mirlitons on a plate (for easier turning). Microwave on **HIGH 20 MINUTES**, rotating plate every 5 minutes. Let stand 5 minutes, then scoop out pulp, and set shells aside. Moisten bread with water and squeeze.

2. Melt fat in a 2 quart dish. Sauté onion, garlic, onion tops and celery on **HIGH 6 MINUTES**. Add moistened bread, mashed up mirliton pulp, egg, salt and pepper. Cook on **HIGH 5 MINUTES**. Stir in shrimp and parsley. Stuff mixture in mirliton shells, sprinkle on bread crumbs and place on a flat plate. Microwave on **HIGH 2 OR 3 MINUTES** until heated through.

STEWED OKRA/okras mijotés

Can be used in Gumbo or served as a vegetable.

Cooking Time: 30 minutes
Utensil: 3 quart casserole
Servings: 4

1 pound frozen or fresh
   okra, sliced
1 cup fresh or drained canned
   tomatoes, chopped
1 cup onion, chopped
2 Tablespoons bacon fat

(It is not necessary
to add water.)

1 teaspoon salt
1/4 teaspoon pepper

1. Place okra, tomatoes, onion and bacon fat in a 3 quart casserole. Cover and microwave on **HIGH 30 MINUTES** (or until okra is tender). Stir once or twice.

2. Season with salt and pepper after cooking.

BAKED ONIONS/oignons au four

Cooking Time: 7 to 8 minutes
Utensil: Glass baking dish
Servings: 4

**4 medium white onions or
8-10 small, peeled
butter
salt and pepper**

Place peeled onions in a glass baking dish. Top each onion with a pat of butter and desired amount of salt and pepper. Cover with plastic wrap. Microwave on **HIGH 7 TO 8 MINUTES**, rotating dish once or twice, until onions are fork tender. Let stand covered 3 minutes.

BAKED POTATOES/pommes de terre au four

Cooking Time: 4 to 12 minutes
Servings: 1-4

Select potatoes of equal size and weight. Scrub skins and pierce with a fork in several places. Place potatoes near the corners and microwave on **HIGH** according to the time chart. Turn and reposition potatoes half way through cooking time. When potato feels slightly soft to the touch, remove and wrap in foil or a terry towel. If there are a few hard spots, roll wrapped potato **LIGHTLY** on the counter top.

Baked Potato	Time on High
1 medium	4-6 minutes
2 medium	8-11 minutes
4 medium	13-15 minutes

GOURMET STUFFED POTATOES
pommes de terre farcies

Cooking Time: 22 minutes
Utensils: 4-cup glass measuring cup
            Glass serving plate
Servings: 8

4 medium baking potatoes

1. Bake potatoes in the Microwave until slightly soft to touch so the skin will stay firm when stuffed. See chart on page 167 for cooking time. Cut hot potatoes in half lengthwise and carefully scoop out pulp. Beat with electric mixer until smooth.

1 cup (8 oz.) sour cream
1/2 teaspoon salt
1/8 teaspoon pepper
1/2 teaspoon Beau Monde seasoning or your favorite

2. Add sour cream, salt, pepper and Beau Monde. Beat until fluffy.

1/4 cup milk

3. Heat milk in microwave **1 MINUTE ON HIGH** and add gradually.

1 (8 oz.) can sliced mushrooms, drained
1/4 cup green onion, chopped
1/4 cup butter

4. In a 4-cup measure, sauté mushrooms and onion in butter on **HIGH 3 MINUTES**. Fold into potato mixture. Fill potato shells.

1/4 cup buttered bread crumbs

5. Sprinkle with bread crumbs. Place on glass serving platter and microwave on **HIGH 2-3 MINUTES** or until heated through. Freezes satisfactorily.

HOT POTATO

Cooking Time: 31 minutes
Utensils: 2 quart baking dish
4-cup measuring cup
Servings: 6-8

4 medium potatoes
1/4 cup water mixed with
1/2 teaspoon salt

1. Peel potatoes and slice thinly into a 2 quart baking dish. Add salt water. Cover. Cook on **HIGH 18 MINUTES,** stirring every 5 minutes. Drain.

3 Tablespoons butter
3 Tablespoons flour
1-3/4 cups milk
2 cups mild cheddar cheese, grated
1 (4 oz.) can green chilies, chopped
1 teaspoon salt
1/2 teaspoon garlic powder

2. In a 4-cup measure, micromelt butter, whisk in flour and add milk gradually. Cook on **HIGH 6 MINUTES,** stirring every 2 minutes until mixture thickens. Add cheese, chilies, salt and garlic powder.

1/2 cup buttered bread crumbs

3. Fold sauce gently into potatoes. Top with buttered bread crumbs. Cover with wax paper and microwave on **HIGH 7 MINUTES.**

SALADE SAVOY
salade savoyarde aux noix et aux lardons

(An unusual, hearty, country style salad from the Savoy Province of France, prepared with a zesty vinaigrette sauce topped with roasted pecans and crisp slab-bacon pieces—compliments of "Bess" Bessmertny.)

Cooking Time: 15 minutes
Utensils: Plat and pie plate
Large salad bowl
Servings: 6

8 cups salad greens, escarole, curly chicory or endive

1. Wash carefully, dry and reserve in the refrigerator in a moist towel.

3 drained fillets of anchovies, cut up and mashed
1 large clove garlic, mashed
1 whole lemon, squeezed (save some lemon to squeeze over apples)
2 Tablespoons wine vinegar
1/2 to 1 teaspoon salt (anchovies will be salty)
1/2 teaspoon milled black pepper
1 sprig of fresh dill, minced
4 Tablespoons good bland oil
1 cup crumbled crisp bacon (approximately 10 slices)
1 cup lightly roasted pecans

2. In a large salad bowl, mash the anchovies and add garlic, lemon, vinegar, salt, pepper, dill (or substitute 4 sprigs of finely chopped chives). Stir well. Add oil and beat with a fork or whisk into an emulsion. Microwave bacon between paper towels on a plate on **HIGH 1 MINUTE** per slice of bacon. Place pecans in a pie plate. Microwave on **HIGH 4-5 MINUTES.** Stir every 2 minutes.

1 cup thinly sliced tart green apples, peeled and cored
2 sprigs parsley, finely chopped

3. Cut salad greens in over-bite-sizes and place on top of the dressing. Sprinkle bacon on top of the salad. Arrange slices of apple on top. Sprinkle on pecans and parsley.

Fifteen minutes before serving, toss salad very thoroughly.

SPINACH AND ARTICHOKE HEARTS
épinards et fonds d'artichauts

Cooking Time: 15 minutes
Utensil: 3 quart casserole
Servings: 6-8

2 teaspoons (or 2 cubes)
of instant beef bouillon
3 (10 oz.) packages frozen
chopped spinach
1/2 teaspoon salt
1/4 teaspoon black pepper
1/4 teaspoon Tabasco

1. Place frozen spinach and bouillon in a 3 quart casserole. Cover. Cook on **HIGH 10 MINUTES** (or until tender). Stir once or twice. Drain. Add salt, pepper and Tabasco.

1/2 pint sour cream
1 (8 oz.) can artichoke
hearts, drained and
quartered
2 Tablespoons margarine

2. Fold in sour cream and artichokes. Dot with margarine. Cover. Cook on **HIGH 5 MINUTES.**

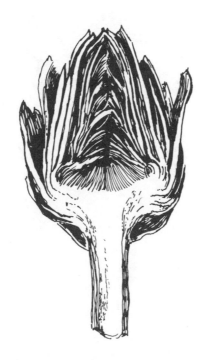

SPINACH WITH ONIONS/épinards aux oignons

Cooking Time: 19 minutes
Utensil: 2 quart casserole
Servings: 8

2 (10 oz.) packages frozen chopped spinach

1. Cook spinach in the box, on **HIGH 14 MINUTES.** Drain. Place in a 2 quart casserole.

1/2 pint sour cream
1 package dry onion soup mix
2 Tablespoons Sherry

2. Add sour cream, onion soup and sherry. Cook on **HIGH 5 MINUTES.**

JALAPENO SQUASH

Cooking Time: 31 minutes
Utensils: 9" x 5" loaf dish
2 quart casserole
Servings: 6

2 cups cooked yellow squash

1. See recipe on page 175. Drain and reserve ¼ cup of liquid. Set aside.

1 (6 oz.) envelope jalapeno corn bread mix
1 egg
2/3 cup milk

2. In a mixing bowl, combine corn bread mix, egg and milk. Place in a greased glass loaf dish (approximately 9" x 5"). Cover with wax paper. Cook on **HIGH 5 MINUTES.** Turn dish once. Test for doneness with a wooden pick. Crumble ½ of the corn bread into a 2 quart casserole.

(Serve remaining corn bread in squares, if desired)

1 egg, beaten
1/4 cup liquid from squash
3 Tablespoons pimento, diced
1 Tablespoon green chili pepper, diced
3/4 cup Colby Longhorn Cheese, grated

3. Mix together egg, liquid, squash, pimento and peppers. Add to crumbled corn bread. Mix well. Top with cheese. Cook on **HIGH 8 MINUTES.** Cover after cooking.

SQUASH AND PINE NUTS

Cooking Time: 33 minutes
Utensils: Browning dish
2 quart dish
4-cup glass measuring cup
Servings: 6-8

1-1/2 pounds pork, ground
1/2 teaspoon salt
1/4 teaspoon cayenne pepper

1. Preheat browning dish on High 4 minutes. Brown meat, season, then cover and cook on **HIGH 5 MINUTES.** Pour off liquid and continue cooking on **HIGH 5 MINUTES.** Drain and set aside.

6 small yellow squash
1 cup onion, sliced
2 Tablespoons water
4 Tablespoons butter
1/2 teaspoon salt

2. Wash and slice squash diagonally. Place squash, onion and water in a 2 quart dish. Cover and microwave on **HIGH 10 MINUTES** or until tender. Drain. Add butter and salt and combine with meat.

4 Tablespoons butter
4 Tablespoons Wondra flour
1-1/2 cups milk
1/2 teaspoon salt
1/4 teaspoon cayenne pepper
1/2 teaspoon allspice
1/4 cup pine nuts or
slivered almonds

3. In a 4-cup measure, melt butter. Whisk in flour and milk. Cook on **HIGH 3 MINUTES.** Stir once. Add salt, pepper and allspice. Pour sauce over meat and squash. Add nuts and cook uncovered on **HIGH 10 MINUTES.** Rotate dish once.

YELLOW SQUASH

Fresh from the garden!

Cooking Time: 18-20 minutes
Utensil: 2 quart dish
Servings: 4 (2 cups)

**4 cups yellow squash,
  sliced or diced
1/2 cup onion, chopped
4 Tablespoons margarine**

Place squash, onion and margarine in a 2 quart dish. Cover with wax paper. Microwave on **HIGH 18-20 MINUTES** or until squash is tender. Stir once or twice.

**(It is not necessary to
  add water.)**

**1 teaspoon salt
1/4 teaspoon white pepper**

Season with salt and pepper.

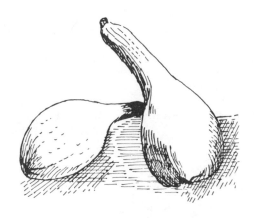

YAM AND APPLE SCALLOP

Cooking Time: 25 minutes
Utensils: Plate
        9" or 10" round dish
Servings: 6

4 medium-size yams cooked or 1 (1 lb.) can, drained
2 medium apples, cored and cut in rings
1 Tablespoon lemon juice

Micro Memo: For cooking whole sweet potatoes

1 potato - 5 to 6 minutes
2 potatoes - 8 to 11 min.
3 potatoes - 12 to 15 min.
4 potatoes - 18 minutes
(pierce potato with fork several times)

1/2 cup brown sugar, firmly packed or 1/4 cup liquid brown sugar
1 teaspoon salt
1/2 teaspoon mace
1/2 teaspoon cinnamon
1/2 cup pecans, chopped
2 Tablespoons butter, melted

1. Wash yams (sweet potatoes), cut in half lengthwise and place, without drying, in a plastic bag. For easier turning, place bagged yams on a plate. Cook on **HIGH 10 MINUTES.** Turn plate once or twice. Peel cooked potatoes and cut in flat, lengthwise slices about ½ inch thick. Arrange a layer of yams in a buttered 9" or 10" round dish. Add a layer of sliced apples; then sprinkle with ½ Tablespoon of lemon juice.

2. Mix together brown sugar, salt, mace, cinnamon and pecans. Cover apples with this mixture and drizzle on half the butter. Repeat layers of potatoes and apples; sprinkle with lemon and cover with remainder of brown sugar mixture. Add remaining butter. Cover with plastic wrap and cook on **HIGH 15 MINUTES.** Turn dish 2 or 3 times.

STEWED ZUCCHINI

Very easy to prepare.

Cooking Time: 20 minutes
Utensil: 4 quart casserole
Servings: 4

**3 medium zucchini, peeled
   and diced
3 fresh tomatoes, diced
1 cup onion, chopped
2 cloves garlic, minced
   (or 1 teaspoon garlic
   powder)
1/4 cup margarine**

**(It is not necessary
   to add water.)**

Place zucchini, tomatoes, onion, garlic and margarine in a 4 quart casserole. Cover with wax paper. Microwave on **HIGH 20 MINUTES.** Stir every 5 minutes.

**1 teaspoon salt
1/4 teaspoon pepper**

Season with salt and pepper after cooking.

ZUCCHINI AUX CHAMPIGNONS

Cooking Time: 14 minutes
Utensil: 3 quart casserole
Servings: 6

2 Tablespoons butter
2 teaspoons parsley
2 Tablespoons onion,
   chopped

1. In a 3 quart casserole, micromelt butter. Add parsley and onion. Sauté on **HIGH 2 MINUTES.**

1/2 pound fresh mushrooms,
   sliced

2. Add mushrooms and sauté on **HIGH 2 MINUTES.**

3 medium zucchini, thinly
   sliced
1 large ripe tomato,
   diced
1 teaspoon salt
1/4 teaspoon cayenne pepper
1/4 teaspoon garlic powder

3. Add zucchini, tomato and seasonings. Cover with wax paper. Cook on **HIGH 5 MINUTES.**

1/2 cup mild cheddar cheese,
   grated
1/2 cup seasoned bread
   crumbs

4. Stir in cheese. Top mixture with bread crumbs. Cover with wax paper. Cook on **HIGH 5 MINUTES.**

ZUCCHINI MAISON

Cooking Time: 21 minutes
Utensils: 8-cup glass measuring cup
2-cup glass measuring cup
3 quart casserole
Servings: 6

**6 medium sized zucchini
sliced about 1/2" thick
1/4 cup water
1/2 teaspoon salt**

1. Place zucchini and water in an 8-cup measure. Cover with wax paper. Cook on **HIGH 15 MINUTES.** Stir once during cooking time. Drain well. Add salt.

**1/2 cup thinly slivered
onions
4 Tablespoons olive oil
2 Tablespoons parsley,
chopped**

2. In a 2-cup measure, sauté onions and parsley in olive oil. Cook on **HIGH 3 MINUTES.**

**2 ripe tomatoes, peeled
and sliced
1/2 teaspoon salt
1/2 teaspoon cayenne pepper
1 teaspoon garlic powder
1/4 teaspoon Italian
seasoning
1/2 cup Parmesan cheese,
grated**

3. To assemble in a 3 quart casserole, place a layer of zucchini, a layer of tomatoes, onion and olive oil, seasonings and Parmesan cheese. Repeat layers ending with Parmesan cheese. Cover. Cook on **HIGH 3 MINUTES.**

ZUCCHINI MOZZARELLA

Cooking Time: 18 minutes
Utensil: 3 quart casserole
Servings: 6

**1-1/2 pounds zucchini,
  sliced
1/4 cup water
1/2 teaspoon salt**

1. Place zucchini and water in a 3 quart casserole. Cover with wax paper. Cook on **HIGH 15 MINUTES.** Stir once during cooking time. Drain. Add salt.

**4 oz. Mozzarella slices
4 oz. tomato sauce
1/4 teaspoon Italian
  seasoning
Parmesan cheese**

2. Place slices of cheese over drained zucchini. Pour tomato sauce and seasoning over cheese and top with Parmesan cheese. Cook on **HIGH 3 MINUTES.**

ZUCCHINI STUFFED TOMATOES
tomates farcies aux zucchini

Cooking Time: 18 minutes
Utensils: 2 quart measuring cup
Round baking dish
Servings: 8

8 medium tomatoes

1. Cut a thin slice from top of each tomato; scoop out pulp (reserve), leaving a ¼ inch shell. Chop pulp.

1/4 cup butter
3 medium zucchini, diced
(about 1 pound)
1 cup onion, chopped
1 teaspoon garlic powder
1/4 teaspoon basil leaves
1/8 teaspoon black pepper

2. Combine, butter, zucchini, onion, garlic, basil, pepper and tomato pulp in a 2 quart dish or measuring cup. Cover with plastic wrap. Cook on **HIGH 10 MINUTES.**

1/2 pound fresh mushrooms,
sliced or 1 (8 oz.) can
sliced mushrooms, drained
1 teaspoon salt
1 cup toasted croutons

3. Add mushrooms, cover and continue cooking on **HIGH 5 MINUTES** (or until zucchini is tender). Stir in salt and croutons.

4. Spoon mixture into tomato shells. Place tomatoes in baking dish and just before serving, microwave on **HIGH 2-3 MINUTES.** Do not overcook tomatoes.

Desserts

Desserts:
    A fine meal is never complete without a special dessert. Cakes, pies, fruits, candies, and puddings cooked in the Microwave in a minimum of time add the pièce de résistance.

CAKES

PIES

FRUIT

CANDY & CUSTARD

ANGEL FLAKE CAKE

Cooking Time: 23 minutes for both cakes
Utensils: 2 quart round glass dish
1 quart round glass dish
Servings: 12

1 (12 oz.) box vanilla
wafers
1 cup butter (2 sticks)
2 cups sugar
6 eggs

1/4 cup milk
7 oz. angel flake coconut
1 teaspoon vanilla
1 cup pecans, finely
chopped

1. Crush vanilla wafers and set aside. Cream butter, add sugar and beat until smooth. Add eggs **one at a time.** These three steps can be done in a food processor.

2. Add milk alternately with crushed wafers and coconut. Add vanilla and nuts. Pour 2/3 of the mixture into a round 2 quart glass dish which has been lined with wax paper. (Crisscross 2 sheets for bottom and sides). Press a small juice glass in the center of cake mixture. Cook on **MEDIUM OR SLO COOK 8 MINUTES.** Rotate dish 2 times. Continue to cook on **HIGH 5 MINUTES.** Rotate dish one or two times for more even cooking. Remove glass, let sit inverted 10 minutes. (Cook the other 1/3 of mixture in a 1 quart round glass dish on **MEDIUM 8 MINUTES** and **HIGH 2 MINUTES.**

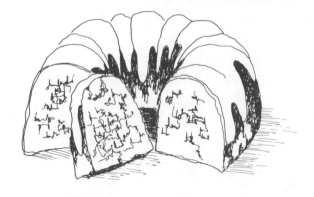

CAJUN FIG CAKE

Cooking Time: 16 minutes 30 seconds
Utensils: 2 cake dishes, 8" round or square
             Glass mixing bowl
Servings: 8

1/2 cup butter
2 cups sugar
3 eggs, slightly beaten

2-1/2 cups flour, all-
**   purpose**
1 teaspoon baking soda
2 cups fig preserves,
**   mashed in mixer**

1. Soften butter in a glass mixing bowl for **30 SECONDS ON HIGH.** Cream butter, sugar and eggs.

2. Add flour, soda and figs. Pour into 2 buttered and floured baking dishes (8" round or square). Microwave each on **HIGH 8 MINUTES,** turning every two minutes.

CHERRY NUT UPSIDE DOWN CAKE

Cooking Time: 10 minutes
Utensil: Round 8" or 9" cake dish (2" deep)
Servings: 8

Preparation of dish:

2 Tablespoons margarine
1/2 cup nuts

1 can cherry pie filling
1 layer plain cake mix (2 cups batter) (make by package directions)

1. Coat sides with margarine. Pat on crushed nuts. Cut circle of wax paper to fit bottom of dish.

2. Pour in pie filling. Top with cake mix batter. Cook on **MEDIUM OR SLO COOK 7 MINUTES.** Turn dish a ¼ turn every 2 minutes. Cook another **3 MINUTES ON HIGH.** Let stand 10 minutes before turning out.

COCA-COLA CAKE/gateau au Coca-Cola

Cooking Time: 14½ minutes (includes icing)
Utensils: 11" x 7" glass dish
2-cup glass measuring cup
4-cup glass measuring cup
Makes 18 squares

CAKE

2 cups all-purpose flour
2 cups sugar
1 cup miniature
marshmallows

1. In a mixing bowl, sift flour and sugar together. Stir in marshmallows.

1/2 cup Crisco
3/4 cup Coke
3 Tablespoons cocoa

2. Put Crisco, Coke and cocoa in a 2-cup glass measure. Heat in Microwave until Crisco melts, **2 MINUTES**. Pour over flour mixture.

1/2 cup buttermilk
1 teaspoon soda
2 eggs, beaten

3. Stir in buttermilk, soda and eggs. Pour into greased glass dish. Cook on **HIGH FOR 11 MINUTES**. Turn dish ¼ every 3 minutes.

(Begin to prepare icing)

ICING

6 Tablespoons margarine
3 Tablespoons cocoa
6 Tablespoons Coke

1. Mix margarine, cocoa and Coke in 4-cup measure. Bring to boil in Microwave—about 1½ **MINUTES**.

2/3 box powdered sugar
3/4 cup broken pecans

2. Pour cocoa mixture over powdered sugar. Add pecans—mix well. Ice while cake is hot.

DEEP DISH PINEAPPLE CRUMBLE

Cooking Time: 10 minutes
Utensil: 2 quart round dish or
          Bundt dish
Servings: 12

2 cups flour, all-purpose
1 cup sugar
1/2 cup butter, softened

1. Mix flour, sugar and butter together with a fork until crumbly.

2 teaspoons cinnamon

2. For crumb topping, remove 1 cup of crumbly mixture, stir in cinnamon and reserve.

2 teaspoons baking powder

3. Stir baking powder into large crumbled mixture.

2 eggs
3/4 cup unsweetened pineapple juice

4. Whisk eggs with pineapple juice and mix lightly into crumb mixture.

5. Lightly grease a 2 quart round casserole or Bundt dish. Pour in mixture and sprinkle on crumb topping. Microwave on **MEDIUM 8 MINUTES,** turning dish once. Cook on **HIGH 2 MINUTES.**

DORA'S BANANA BREAD

Try whipped cream on top.

Cooking Time: 13 minutes
Utensil: 2 quart glass casserole or a Bundt dish
Servings: 12

1/2 cup butter 1-1/2 cups sugar 2 eggs, beaten	1. Cream butter and sugar in a 2 quart casserole. Add eggs, mixing well.
1-1/2 cups flour, all-purpose 1/2 teaspoon mace 3/4 teaspoon baking soda	2. Blend in flour, mace and soda.
3 Tablespoons buttermilk 1 cup ripe bananas, mashed 1 teaspoon vanilla	3. Beat in buttermilk, bananas and vanilla. Level mixture in a 2 quart dish or a Bundt dish. Microwave on **MEDIUM 8 MINUTES**, rotating dish 2 times, and then on **HIGH 5 MINUTES**. Let cake stand 5 minutes (center will be moist from bananas, but do not overcook). Keep cake moist in plastic wrap after cooking.

STRAWBERRY CAKE/gateau à la fraise

Cooking Time: 12 minutes
Utensil: Bundt pan or 3 quart casserole
Servings: 16 slices

1 box white cake mix
1 (3 oz.) box strawberry
   jello

1. Mix together cake mix and jello.

3 eggs, well beaten
1/2 cup vegetable oil
1/2 cup milk
1 (10 oz.) box strawberries,
   defrosted and drained
   (reserve 1/2 cup juice
   for icing)
1 teaspoon vanilla

2. Blend in eggs, oil, milk, straw-berries and vanilla. Pour mixture into a microwave safe Bundt pan or a 3 quart casserole dish. If using the casserole, place a piece of wax paper in bottom of dish. After pouring in mixture, place a juice glass in the center. Cook on **MEDI-UM 8 MINUTES.** Turn dish 2 times. Cook on **HIGH 3 MIN-UTES.** Let cool 5 minutes, remove glass and turn out on plate. Cool cake in refrigerator before icing.

STRAWBERRY ICING

1 pound box powdered
   sugar, sifted
1/2 cup butter, melted
1/2 cup strawberry juice
1 teaspoon vanilla

Micromelt butter on **HIGH 1 MIN-UTE.** Add sugar, juice and vanilla. Stir until blended—pour over cooled cake.

STRAWBERRY ROUND BREAD/pain à la fraise

Try whipped cream on top for dessert—plain for breakfast.

Cooking Time: 10 minutes
Utensil: 2 quart round casserole with high sides
Servings: 16

1/2 (3 oz.) package Strawberry jello
1-1/2 cups flour, all-purpose
1 cup sugar
1/2 teaspoon cinnamon
1/4 teaspoon salt
1/2 teaspoon soda

1. Sift together jello, flour, sugar, cinnamon, salt and soda.

2 eggs, well beaten
3/4 cup vegetable oil
1/2 cup chopped nuts
1 (10 oz.) package frozen strawberries, defrosted

2. In another bowl, combine eggs, oil, nuts and strawberries. Stir in dry ingredients and mix well with spoon.

3. Pour into dish lined on the bottom with wax paper. Cook on **MEDIUM OR SLO COOK 7 MINUTES.** Turn the dish 2 times. Cook on **HIGH 3 MINUTES** or until wooden pick comes out clean.

SPICE SNACKIN' CAKE

Cooking Time: 9 minutes
Utensil: 5" x 9" glass dish
Servings: 6

14 oz. box of Spice
   Snackin' Cake Mix
   (any flavor may be
   substituted)
3/4 cup water

1. Mix as directed on box, using only 3/4 cup water. Place in a 5" x 9" buttered glass dish or cut a piece of wax paper to fit bottom.

2. Microwave on **MEDIUM 6 MINUTES**; rotate dish one time. Cook on **HIGH 3 MINUTES**; rotate dish one time.

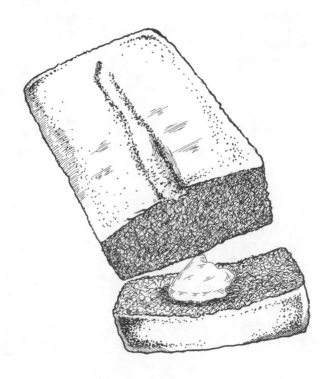

SYRUP CAKE/gateau au sirop

Cooking Time: 9 minutes
Utensil: 9" Bundt dish or a
        2 quart round casserole
Servings: 8

2 cups flour, all-purpose
1 teaspoon baking powder
1 teaspoon baking soda
pinch of salt
1/2 cup butter, melted

1. Combine flour, baking powder, salt and soda in a mixing bowl. Stir in melted butter.

2 eggs, beaten
1/4 cup milk
1-1/2 cup heavy dark syrup
    or molasses

2. Mix together eggs, milk and syrup. Add to flour mixture and blend well with beater. Line bottom of a microsafe 9" Bundt dish or a round 2 quart casserole dish with wax paper. Pour in mixture. Microwave on **MEDIUM 6 MINUTES**; turning dish one time. Continue to microwave on **HIGH 3 MINUTES**. Let cake stand 5 minutes before turning out.

Micro Memo:

    To make a bundt dish, place an empty juice glass in center of mixture in the 2 quart casserole. Twist glass to remove after cooking.

193

DOUBLE PIE CRUST

Cooking Time: 6 minutes for each crust
Utensil: 9" glass pie plate
Makes 2-9" pie crusts

2-3/4 cups flour, all-purpose
1-1/2 teaspoons salt
1 cup shortening
1 egg
ice water

Blend shortening, flour and salt. Beat egg in a measuring cup and add enough ice water to measure 1/2 cup liquid. Add liquid to flour and shortening. Knead 5 times and form 2 balls. Wrap in wax paper and refrigerate at least 15 minutes. Roll out dough and shape in a 9" pie plate. Prick bottom and sides with a fork. Microwave **6 MINUTES ON HIGH** until crust is flaky. Rotate plate several times.

OATMEAL PIE CRUST

Cooking Time: 6 minutes for each crust
Utensil: Glass pie plate
Makes double crust for 9" pie

1-1/2 cups unsifted all-
     purpose flour
1 teaspoon salt
1/2 cup vegetable
     shortening
3/4 cup uncooked oats
7 Tablespoons cold water

Combine flour and salt. Cut mixture into shortening until it resembles coarse crumbs. Stir in oats. Sprinkle with water by tablespoonfuls, mixing until dry ingredients are moistened. Form into ball. Roll out on floured board and press into pie plate. Prick lightly with a fork. Microwave on **HIGH 6 MINUTES** or until flaky. Rotate plate two times.

FRENCH PASTRY/croûte de tarte

Cooking Time: 5-6 minutes
Utensil: Glass pie plate
Makes 1—9" or 10" shell

1-1/2 cups all-purpose
   flour, sifted
1/2 cup butter
1 egg yolk
1/2 teaspoon salt
2-1/2-3 Tablespoons cold
   water

Mix flour, butter, egg yolk and salt together with fingers until coarse and crumbly. Add cold water until a ball forms. Dough may also be made in a food processor. Knead 5 times, wrap in wax paper and chill at least 30 minutes. Roll out the dough, line it into the glass plate, prick lightly with a fork, flute the edges and chill again until firm. Microwave on **HIGH 5-6 MIN-UTES** or until flaky. Rotate plate two times.

FROZEN PIE CRUST

Cooking Time: 4 or 5 minutes
Utensil: Glass pie plate
Makes 1 — 9" shell

9" frozen prepared pie
   crust

(Remove frozen shell from foil
   pan to a 9" glass pie plate.)

Press crust into place after it thaws. Prick lightly with a fork. Microwave on **HIGH 4 OR 5 MINUTES** until crust appears flaky. Rotate dish one time.

195

ALMOND PEAR PIE/tarte de poires à la Normande

An elegant dessert from France!

Cooking Time: 12 minutes
Utensil: 9" or 10" glass pie plate
Servings: 8

FOR PIE PASTRY
1-1/2 cups all-purpose flour
1/2 cup butter
1 egg yolk
1/2 teaspoon salt
2-1/2 - 3 Tablespoons cold
     water

FOR THE FRANGIPANE
1/3 cup butter
1/3 cup sugar
1 egg, beaten
1 egg yolk
2 teaspoons kirsch
1/2 cup almonds, ground
2 Tablespoons flour

TO FINISH
3-4 ripe pears
granulated sugar (for sprinkling)
1/2 cup apricot preserves,
     warmed

1. Make the pastry dough and chill at least 30 minutes. Roll out, line pie plate and prick lightly with a fork. Chill again. Cook on **HIGH 5 MINUTES**, rotating plate every 2 minutes. Chill.

2. Cream the butter, gradually beat in the sugar and continue beating until mixture is light and soft. Gradually add egg and yolk, beating well. Add the kirsch, then stir in the ground almonds and flour. Pour the frangipane into the chilled pastry, spreading it evenly.

3. Peel the pears, halve them and scoop out the cores and stem fiber. Cut them crosswise in very thin slices. Lift sliced pear with knife and arrange on the frangipane in a wheel pattern. Press pears down gently until they touch the pastry dough base. Sprinkle sugar over pears. Cover pie with wax paper and microwave on **HIGH 7 MINUTES**, turning every 2 minutes. Brush pie with apricot preserves and serve at room temperature.

196

APPLE CRUMB PIE

Cooking Time: 10-12 minutes
Utensils: Glass mixing bowl
 9" glass pie plate
Servings: 6

1/2 cup butter
1/4 cup sugar
2 cups graham cracker
 crumbs

1. Melt butter on **HIGH 1 MINUTE** in a glass mixing bowl. Stir in sugar and crumbs, mix well. Press firmly half of mixture to line a 9" glass pie plate.

5 cups thinly sliced
 apples (4-6 medium)
1/2 cup sugar
1 teaspoon cinnamon

2. Place apple slices (¼" thick) piled high in crumb-lined pie plate and sprinkle with sugar mixed with cinnamon.

 Use remaining crumbs to mold around apples, leaving center top open. Cover pie with wax paper. Microwave on **HIGH 10-12 MINUTES.** Let stand covered 10 minutes.

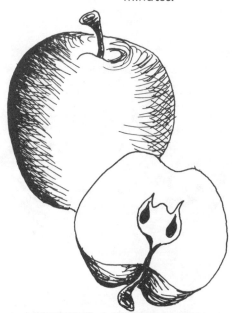

197

DOUBLE CRUST APPLE PIE
tarte de pommes en croûte

Cooking Time: 10 minutes
Utensil: 9" glass pie plate
Servings: 6

1-9" baked pie crust*
   in a glass dish
1 Tablespoon flour

1. Sprinkle 1 Tablespoon flour on baked crust.

8 apples, peeled, cored
   and sliced
1 cup sugar
4 Tablespoons flour
1/2 teaspoon salt
1/2 teaspoon nutmeg
1/2 teaspoon cinnamon

*Double Crust Pastry
   recipe is on page 194

2. Toss apples in sugar, flour, salt, nutmeg and cinnamon mixture until well coated. Fill baked crust with apples to the top of shell. Roll out dough for the top crust* and cut to the size of an inverted 9" pie plate. Place over apples, seal edges and cut a design in top crust for steam vents. Cook on **HIGH 10 MINUTES.** For a browner crust, sprinkle on a mixture of cinnamon and sugar.

BANANA CREAM PIE/tarte à la crème de banane

Cooking Time: 12 minutes
Utensil: 2 quart glass bowl
Servings: 6

9" micro baked pie crust*
2 bananas, sliced

1. Place sliced bananas in cooled crust.

2/3 cup sugar
3-1/2 Tablespoons cornstarch
1/2 teaspoon salt
2 cups milk

2. In a 2 quart glass bowl, mix together sugar, cornstarch and salt. Stir milk in gradually and cook on **HIGH 10 MINUTES.** Stir frequently.

3 egg yolks, slightly
     beaten

3. Stir small amount of hot liquid into eggs then return eggs to hot liquid. Cook on **HIGH 2 MINUTES.**

1 Tablespoon butter
1-1/2 teaspoons vanilla
1/2 teaspoon banana
     flavoring

4. Add butter, vanilla and banana flavoring. Pour over bananas. When cool, top with whipped cream.

*Pastry recipes are on pages
   ~94 & 195

Variation: For Vanilla Cream Pie, omit bananas and banana flavoring.

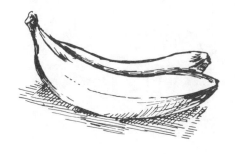

BROWNIE PIE

Cooking Time: 12 minutes
Utensils: 4-cup glass measuring cup
2 quart round dish
Servings: 12

2 squares unsweetened
chocolate
1/3 cup butter
1 cup sugar
2 eggs, lightly beaten

3/4 cup flour, all-purpose
1/4 teaspoon baking powder
1/4 teaspoon salt
1 teaspoon vanilla
1/2 cup chopped nuts

1. Place chocolate and butter in a 4-cup measure. Cook on **MEDIUM 1½ TO 2 MINUTES.** Stir in sugar. Stir a small amount of hot mixture into eggs; return to hot mixture.

2. Stir in flour, baking powder, salt, vanilla and nuts. Spread in a 2 quart round dish, lightly greased.

3. Cook on **MEDIUM OR SLO COOK 7 MINUTES.** Turn dish 2 times, then cook on **HIGH 3 MINUTES.** When cool, cut into wedges.

CHOCOLATE PIE/tarte au chocolat

Kids love to make this—and eat it, too!

Cooking Time: 7-8 minutes
Utensils: 9" glass pie plate
          4-cup glass measuring cup
Servings: 8

9" crumb crust or pie shell (see pages 194 & 195 for recipes)

1. Prepare crust or shell and place in a 9" pie plate.

**1 (5¼ oz.) package chocolate pudding and pie filling
2 cups milk**

2. Mix pudding with milk in a 4-cup measure. Cook on **HIGH 7-8 MINUTES,** stirring often. Pour into pie crust.

3. Refrigerate one hour. Top with a whipped dessert topping when cool.

Micro Memo:

For recipes requiring frequent stirring, leave wooden spoon in dish.

PEACH CRISP/pêches croûstillantes

Fresh peaches in a crunchy crust.

Cooking Time: 3 minutes—pie crust
Utensil: 9" glass pie plate
Servings: 8

VANILLA WAFER CRUST

1-1/4 cups vanilla wafer
  crumbs
5 Tablespoons butter,
  melted

1. Melt butter in a **9"** glass pie plate on **HIGH 1 MINUTE.** Stir in crumbs. Press crumb mixture against bottom and sides of pie plate. Microwave on **HIGH 2 MINUTES,** turning dish once. Chill.

PEACH FILLING

1 (9 oz.) carton Cool Whip
1 (14 oz.) can condensed milk
1/2 cup lemon juice
2 pints of fresh sliced
  peaches (strawberries may
  be substituted)

2. Blend together Cool Whip, condensed milk and lemon juice. Fold in fruit. Pour into crust and chill.

STRAWBERRY KIRSCH PIE

tarte de fraises au kirsch

Cooking Time: 10 minutes
Utensils: 9" pie plate
        8-cup measuring cup
Servings: 8

9" pastry shell	1. Cook pastry shell according to directions on page 195.
4 cups fresh strawberries 1/2 cup powdered sugar, sifted	2. Sprinkle sugar on 3 cups of large, whole strawberries. Set aside one half hour.
1/2 cup water 2 Tablespoons Kirsch 2 Tablespoons Strawberry Liqueur	3. Crush the remaining 1 cup strawberries in an 8-cup measure. Add water. Cook on **HIGH 2 MINUTES**. Press through a sieve. Return juice to 8-cup measure. Add Kirsch and Strawberry Liqueur to juice.
2 Tablespoons cornstarch 1/2 cup sugar	4. Mix cornstarch and sugar together. Stir in small amount of berry juice until smooth—then return to juice in 8-cup measure. Cook on **HIGH 8 MINUTES** or until mixture thickens. Stir once or twice.

Fill pastry shell with the large sugared berries. Pour hot strawberry syrup over berries. Cool in refrigerator. Spoon fluffy dessert topping around outer edge of pie.

RED HOT APPLES/pommes brûlantes

Cooking Time: 12 minutes
Utensil: Deep round dish or
        square glass dish
Servings: 4

1 cup pineapple juice
1/4 cup red hots
3 or 4 shakes red food
coloring
1/4 cup sugar or 1 teaspoon
artificial sweetener

1. Heat juice, red hots, coloring and sugar in a deep casserole on **HIGH 2 MINUTES.**

4 winesap apples

2. Core apples from stem to within ½" of end. Remove 1 inch of skin around stem. Place cut side down in red syrup. Cover with plastic wrap and microwave on **HIGH 2 MINUTES.** Turn apples over—baste and cover. Cook on **HIGH 8 MIN-UTES.**

1/4 cup pecans
1/4 cup raisins
1/4 cup small marshmallows

3. Fill centers of hot apples with nuts, raisins and marshmallows. Cover and let stand 5 minutes.

Micro Memo:

Allow at least 2 minutes cooking time per apple.

BANANAS FOSTER/bananes foster

Cooking Time: 6 minutes 45 seconds
Utensils: 8″ square glass dish
                1-cup glass measuring cup
Servings: 4-6

1/4 cup butter, melted
4 Tablespoons brown sugar
  or 2 Tablespoons liquid
  brown sugar
1-1/2 Tablespoons cinnamon

1. In an 8″ square dish, melt butter. Stir in brown sugar and cinnamon. Bring to a boil on **HIGH 3-4 MINUTES.** Stir at 1 minute intervals.

4 bananas, split and
  quartered
3 Tablespoons banana
  liqueur
1/3 cup rum, heated
vanilla ice cream

2. Add bananas, coating all sides with syrup. Microwave on **HIGH 2 MINUTES.** Add banana liqueur. Heat rum in a 1-cup measure on **HIGH 45 SECONDS.** Pour over bananas and ignite. Serve over vanilla ice cream.

PEARS IN RED WINE/poires au vin rouge
From Paris

Cooking Time: 12 minutes
Utensil: Loaf dish or 2 quart dish
Servings: 4 or 8

4-8 firm pears

1/2 cup sugar
1 cup red wine
1-1/2 cups water
strip of lemon peel
2" piece cinnamon stick
a few drops red food
    coloring

CHANTILLY CREAM

3/4 cup cream
2 teaspoons sugar
1/2 teaspoon vanilla
(Mix together until blended)

BURGUNDY SAUCE

1/2 cup sour cream
1/2 cup plain yogurt
3 Tablespoons red wine
    syrup (cooked with
    pears)
(Mix together until blended)

1. Choose a dish (loaf dish for 4 or round 2 quart casserole for 8) that just fits the pears when standing upright. In the dish, place sugar, red wine, water, lemon peel, red coloring and cinnamon. Amount will be the same for 4 or 8 pears. Microwave on **HIGH 5 MINUTES** or until mixture boils. Let cool slightly.

2. Peel pears, remove the 'eye' from the base but leave the stalk. Immerse pears in syrup. Cover with wax paper or a lid and microwave on **HIGH 7 MINUTES**. Pears will be tender, but not mushy when done. Serve with either Chantilly Cream or Burgundy Sauce.

HOT FRUIT MEDLEY/pot-pourri aux fruits

Cooking Time: 25 minutes
Utensil: 3 quart casserole
Servings: 8

1 (16 oz.) can pear halves
1 (16 oz.) can apricot halves
1 (16 oz.) can cling peach
   halves
1 (16 oz.) can pineapple
   chunks
juice of 2 oranges
zest of 1 orange or 1
   lemon
1 (8 oz.) package pitted
   dates, chopped

Drain fruit and place 1/3 cup of juice from each can in a 3 quart casserole along with orange juice and zest (grated rind). Cook on **HIGH 20 MINUTES** until liquid is reduced by half. Add fruit and dates. Cook on **HIGH 5 MINUTES.** Serve in compotes for dessert.

RUBY'S VANILLA ICE CREAM
crème glace à la vanille

·Cooking Time: 28 minutes
Utensil: 4 quart dish
Servings: 12

1/2 gallon milk
2 (13 oz.) cans evaporated
milk

1. Heat milk in a 4 quart dish on **HIGH 15 MINUTES.** Stir once or twice.

6 eggs, beaten
1-1/2 cups sugar
2 Tablespoons cornstarch
1/4 teaspoon salt

2. Mix eggs, sugar, cornstarch and salt with electric mixer until thick. Add small amount of hot milk to mixture then return mixture to hot milk and mix well. Microwave on **HIGH 13 MINUTES.** Stir at 3 minute intervals.

3 Tablespoons vanilla

3. Add vanilla and cool in the refrigerator. Mixture is ready for freezing.

VARIATIONS:

add 1 (20 oz.) can crushed pineapple
  or 1 (8 oz.) jar cherries, cut up
  or 1 (10 oz.) package frozen strawberries, cut up
  or 2 cups fresh peaches, sliced thinly
reduce vanilla to 1 Tablespoon

BREAD PUDDING/pudding au pain

With Rum Sauce.

Cooking Time: 12 minutes
Utensils: 9" round glass dish
4-cup glass measuring cup
2-cup glass measuring cup
Servings: 8

6 slices white bread, torn in small pieces (crust, too)	1. Place bread in a 9" round glass dish.
2 cups milk 1 Tablespoon margarine	2. Heat milk and margarine on **HIGH 3 MINUTES** in a 4-cup measure.
2 eggs, beaten 1-1/4 cups sugar 1/4 teaspoon salt 1/2 teaspoon cinnamon 1 teaspoon vanilla 1/2 cup raisins	3. Stir small amount of hot milk into beaten eggs. Return eggs to milk. Add sugar, salt, cinnamon, vanilla and raisins. Pour mixture over bread pieces. Cook on **HIGH 7 MINUTES.** Cook 2 minutes longer if center is not firm.

RUM SAUCE

1/4 cup margarine 1/2 cup sugar 2 Tablespoons rum	Mix sugar and rum together in a 2-cup measure. Add margarine. Cook on **HIGH 2 MINUTES.** Serve warm over bread pudding.

CHOCOLATE DELIGHTS

Cooking Time: 2 minutes
Utensil: 2 quart dish
Makes 3 dozen

8 oz. package semi-sweet chocolate squares
1 (14 oz.) can sweetened condensed milk
2 cups pecans, chopped
pinch of salt

1. Melt chocolate on **HIGH 2 MINUTES** in a 2 quart dish. Stir in milk, pecans and salt.

2. Drop by teaspoonful onto wax paper. After candy is hard, carefully turn with a spatula or knife and let underside harden.

TOUT de SUITE PRALINES

Cooking Time: 13 minutes
Utensil: 4 or 5 quart glass or
ceramic dish
Makes 5½ dozen

3/4 cup buttermilk
2 cups sugar
2 cups pecan halves
1/8 teaspoon salt
2 Tablespoons butter

1. Stir together buttermilk, sugar, pecans, salt and butter in a 4 or 5 quart dish. Cook on **HIGH 12 MINUTES**, stirring at 4 minute intervals.

1 teaspoon baking soda

2. Stir in baking soda until foamy. Cook on **HIGH 1 MINUTE**. (This last step gives the pralines a caramel color.) Beat mixture until tacky (about 1 minute). Drop by teaspoonful on a sheet of foil.

CARAMEL CUSTARD/flan

Cooking Time: 21 minutes
Utensils: 1½ quart glass casserole
2-cup glass measuring cup
Servings: 6

1/4 cup sugar
3 eggs
2 egg yolks
1/3 cup sugar

1. Place 1/4 cup sugar in a 1½ quart glass casserole. Microwave on **HIGH 9 MINUTES,** stirring once or twice until the sugar has melted into a dark rich syrup. Coat the bottom and sides of the dish with the syrup. In a small bowl, stir the eggs, yolks and 1/3 cup sugar together until mixed.

2 cups milk, heated
1 teaspoon vanilla

2. In a 2-cup glass measuring cup, heat the milk on **HIGH 4 MINUTES** until simmering. Slowly stir the hot milk into the egg mixture. Add vanilla, then pour into the caramel lined bowl. Cook on **MEDIUM OR SLO COOK 8 MINUTES.** Rotate dish at 2 minute intervals. The center of the custard will still wiggle, but will become firm as it cools. After chilling custard, turn out onto a serving dish.

FRENCH CUSTARD/crème brûlée

With a dark caramel sauce.

Cooking Time: 24 minutes
Utensils: 6 glass custard molds
          4-cup glass measuring cup
Servings: 6

1/2 cup sugar

1. Place sugar in a 4-cup glass measure. Microwave on **HIGH 9-10 MINUTES** until sugar turns dark caramel and bubbles. Stir and quickly pour into 6 individual glass or ceramic molds. Turn dishes to coat bottom and sides. Cool until caramel hardens.

1 (14 oz.) can sweetened
    condensed milk
1 cup whole milk, warmed
3 whole eggs
3 egg yolks
1/2 teaspoon almond extract
1 teaspoon vanilla

2. Combine condensed milk, whole milk, eggs, egg yolks, almond and vanilla in blender 8-10 seconds. Pour into caramelized dishes. Microwave 3 custards at a time on **MEDIUM 6-7 MINUTES.** Turn dishes once or twice. Custard should be firm, but wiggle in center when cooked.

When custard cools, turn out onto serving plates.

FUDGE, "TOUT de SUITE"
fondant, tout de suite

Cooking Time: 2 minutes
Utensil: 8-cup glass measuring cup
Servings: 25 small squares

1 pound powdered sugar
1/2 cup cocoa
1/4 cup milk
1/2 cup butter

1. Blend sugar and cocoa in an 8-cup measure. Add milk and butter. DO NOT STIR! Microwave on **HIGH 2 MINUTES.**

1 Tablespoon vanilla
1/2 cup chopped nuts*

2. Remove from Microwave and stir well to mix. Add vanilla and nuts. Stir until blended. Pour into a greased (use butter wrapper for this purpose) dish of any size and place in the freezer for 20 minutes or refrigerator 1 hour. Cut and serve.

*A variation in the recipe is to substitute 1/2 cup crunchy peanut butter in place of nuts.

HOT FUDGE SAUCE/sauce fondante

Cooking Time: 6 minutes
Utensil: 8-cup glass measuring cup
Makes 4 cups

2 cups sugar
1/2 cup cocoa
1/4 cup light corn syrup
3/4 cup evaporated milk

1 Tablespoon butter
1 teaspoon vanilla
1/8 teaspoon salt
1/2 cup chopped nuts,
(if desired)

1. Mix sugar, cocoa, corn syrup and milk in an 8-cup measure. Cook on **HIGH 6 MINUTES.** Stir every 2 minutes.

2. Add butter, vanilla, salt and nuts. Stir and mix well. Sauce can be stored in a jar in refrigerator. Remove lid and heat in the microwave to return to original consistency.

PEANUT BRITTLE

In 9 minutes!

Cooking Time: 9 minutes
Utensils: 8-cup glass measuring cup
         Flexible cookie sheet
Makes about 1 pound

1 cup raw peanuts*
1 cup granulated sugar
1/2 cup white corn syrup
1/8 teaspoon salt

1. Stir together peanuts, sugar, syrup and salt in an 8-cup measure. Place in microwave and cook on **HIGH** **7-8 MINUTES,** stirring well after 4 minutes. (Wooden spoon can be left in bowl.)

1 teaspoon butter or
    margarine
1 teaspoon vanilla extract

2. Add butter and vanilla to syrup, blending well. Return to microwave and cook **1 MINUTE MORE.** Peanuts will be lightly browned and syrup **very hot.**

1 teaspoon baking soda

3. Add baking soda and gently stir until light and foamy. Pour and spread mixture quickly onto lightly greased (flexible) cookie sheet; let cool one half hour. When cool, break into small pieces. (May be stored in air-tight container.)

*If roasted salted peanuts are used, omit salt and add peanuts after first 4 minutes of cooking.

Variation: 1 cup pecan halves or 1 cup sesame seeds may be substituted for peanuts after the first 4 minutes of cooking.

The following friends submitted recipes which were developed and converted to microwave cooking:

"Bess" Bessmertny

Gerald Breaux

Clarice Burch

Jill Chance

Kurt Cheramie

Beverly Christina

Elise Dalferes

Cathy DeJean

Dave Domingue

Doreen Duhe

Dora Durkee

Felicia Elsbury

Sissy Freeman

Elizabeth Gauthier

Ruby Gueno

Anita G. Guidry

Louise Hanchey

Guyell Harrison

Billie Hebert

Marilyn Heffner

Peggy Henderson

Marilyn Hoffpauir

Verlie House

Millard Ingram

Marty Johnson

Lucy Kellner

Patsy Kincaid

Patty Kuebler

Yvonne Landry

Mary Larson

Beverly Latimer

Jolene Levermann

Pat Link

Delores Melton

LaDonna Norman

Sandy Oliver

Calva Ortego

Ruth Patrick

Linda Prot

Nelson Sapp

Mary Kathryn Scott

Samantha Shields

Kathy Shorey

Dot Smith

Betty Walker

Dorothy Warren

Carolyn Wright

Index

TOUT de SUITE à la MICROWAVE, INC.
P.O. BOX 30121   **LAFAYETTE, LA. 70503**

Please send me _____ copies of **TOUT de SUITE à la MICROWAVE I** @ $9.95 ea. _____

Please send me _____ copies of **TOUT de SUITE à la MICROWAVE II** @ $9.95 ea. _____

Plus postage and handling @ $1.50 per book _____

(Louisiana residents add applicable tax.) _____

Enclosed is my check ☐ or money order ☐ . . . . TOTAL _____
Make checks payable to **TOUT de SUITE.**
No C.O.D.s. Sorry, no foreign checks or currency accepted.

PLEASE PRINT OR TYPE

NAME _____

ADDRESS _____

CITY _____STATE _____ ZIP _____

TOUT de SUITE à la MICROWAVE, INC.
P.O. BOX 30121   **LAFAYETTE, LA. 70503**

Please send me _____ copies of **TOUT de SUITE à la MICROWAVE I** @ $9.95 ea. _____

Please send me _____ copies of **TOUT de SUITE à la MICROWAVE II** @ $9.95 ea. _____

Plus postage and handling @ $1.50 per book _____

(Louisiana residents add applicable tax.) _____

Enclosed is my check ☐ or money order ☐ . . . . TOTAL _____
Make checks payable to **TOUT de SUITE.**
No C.O.D.s. Sorry, no foreign checks or currency accepted.

PLEASE PRINT OR TYPE

NAME _____

ADDRESS _____

CITY _____ STATE _____ ZIP _____

TOUT de SUITE à la MICROWAVE, INC.
P.O. BOX 30121   **LAFAYETTE, LA. 70503**

Please send me _____ copies of **TOUT de SUITE à la MICROWAVE I** @ $9.95 ea. _____

Please send me _____ copies of **TOUT de SUITE à la MICROWAVE II** @ $9.95 ea. _____

Plus postage and handling @ $1.50 per book _____

(Louisiana residents add applicable tax.) _____

Enclosed is my check ☐ or money order ☐ . . . . TOTAL _____
Make checks payable to **TOUT de SUITE.**
No C.O.D.s. Sorry, no foreign checks or currency accepted.

PLEASE PRINT OR TYPE

NAME _____

ADDRESS _____

CITY _____STATE _____ ZIP _____